What Is Web Analytics and How to Get Started

John Cassidy Jr.

ISBN:147507400X
ISBN-13:9781475074000

CONTENTS

FOREWORD

When I started my career working within the digital space, I often encountered small business owners who labeled the Internet as "just a fad". Many of those same business owners did not have a web site and some, believe it or not, did not even have a computer! In addition, representatives from various, local print publications would rail against its use arguing vehemently against the business value of the world wide web versus their own, traditional media vehicle.

Over the last decade and a half, the climate has dramatically changed and the Internet is now an integral part of any organization's operations. Whether it is to generate sales, inform customers, develop new relationships or to simply entertain, few would argue against the importance of having a web presence. Organizations of all sizes, from sole proprietorships, to multinational corporations expend resources or dedicate time to build their presence within this digital world. The Internet has proven to be a boon to business and entrepreneurship expanding the reach of companies both large and small. Even not-for-profit organizations have taken advantage and recognize their web presence as a key element in achieving their own goals and objectives.

Of course, all of this does come with some cost. Despite the influx of free building services and tools, a truly effective, professional web site does cost money to build. Getting users to visit the created pages does not happen on its own. Application of concerted effort and technical know-how is required. The emergence of social media as a crucial piece to a digital presence requires its own, significant resource allocation. Plus, as new technologies emerge, the complexities and subsequent funds attributed to any organization's web presence are sure to increase.

It is likely that you are already well aware of all that I mentioned above. Also, in case you were now wondering, I can assure you that this book is not a lesson in the importance of having a digital presence or on the history of how the Internet came to where it is today. I feel safe in the assumption that describing these things in detail is not necessary these days. I am merely establishing the notion that an organization's web presence represents an important aspect of its operations, whether to make a profit or meet some other objective or series of objectives. In addition, a web site, as part of a wider online presence, represents an investment of time, money and resources that necessitates the use of observation and measurement in order to improve its contribution relative to its organization's goals. In other words, the application of web analytics is a necessary and critical aspect in managing your organization's digital assets and resources through performance measurement and analysis.

INTRODUCTION

Control Through Measurement

Simply stated, we view web analytics as the observation and measurement of activity within an online asset; most commonly, an organization's web site. Web analytics provides you with the ability to collect, measure and analyze activities of online visitors. Furthermore, through measurement of this activity you are able to develop a better understanding of it and ultimately, a better ability to control it. You seek to arrive in a position that will allow you to maintain or improve your web site's performance both now and in the future.

Generally speaking, users visit a web site to locate something they need. The web site provides a system of pages that they can navigate in order to arrive at their intended destination, whether it is an article, a product, a form or some means of contacting an organization. Having the understanding of how this occurs and what factors are influencing it allows you to gain better insights into how a user interacts with your web site. With that insight, you gain more control over your desired outcomes and can seek out improvements to the user's experience and improve the effectiveness and performance of your online presence.

What is measured by any given web site is largely determined by its nature and purpose.   When providing online content, web analytics can be used to determine how deep into a site users typically go and how often they revisit. When selling products online, analytics can be employed to find out how long it takes to close a sale online. Regardless, important actions and activities performed by users can be identified as key contributors to an organization's goals and objectives and employed to enhance your control over and influence of the activities and outcomes your site was designed to generate. A common quote in business states that what is measured can be controlled. We do not pay attention unless we are actively judging performance through concerted, measurement efforts. We can only seek to control our desired outcomes through such endeavors.

What We Seek To Learn Through Measurement and Analysis

Control of desired outcomes. Understanding of user activities. Measuring performance against site objectives and goals. All correctly argued as reasons why we employ web analytics but do they hold any meaning to you? Instead of pondering that question, let's ask ourselves a series of questions:

Do you want to know where your site visitors are coming from?

Do you care how much time users are spending on your site?

Do you know what your most popular products are?

What do your site customers want?

How any people are actually coming to your site?

How relevant is your site's content?

Why are users leaving the site before interacting with it?

Why has your traffic grown stagnant?

Did your new mobile app or Facebook page make any difference?

Was that change implemented across the site's architecture worth the effort?

How are users finding our products within the site?

Are they purchasing products on our site? If not, why?

Why has no one filled out our registration form?

Do users return to the site after their initial visit?

Did our advertising campaign have an impact on site traffic?

How did our newsletter perform?

How is your site actually performing and what are the most important indicators?

Do you know the answers to all of these questions? Are there more that come to mind that are not even listed? Whether or not you can quickly answer these or other, similar questions, how confident are you that your answer is correct? Does it truly explain the what, why or how? Web analytics is intended to answer such questions through careful collection and analysis of relevant data. In turn, your answers to these and other questions concerning your web site's performance represent a solid understanding of the true nature of results and limit any second guessing by supporting assertions with live data. In short, web analytics is intended to support the making of business related decisions as they pertain to your organization's ongoing, digital efforts.

Common Challenges Associated With Web Analytics

By now, you understand why web analytics is important and that you need to measure the performance of your site. It is likely you knew this before you began reading this book. So what might be holding you back? There are several common challenges that are encountered which prevent an individual from getting started or performing web analytics functions properly. So what are they?

Common Misunderstandings

More often than not, such challenges relate to common misunderstandings associated with web analytics. The following list of statements may apply to some that you may have encountered:

"I have too much data"

"My reports are not helpful"

"I do not trust the data that I have"

"I have a web analytics tool but...."

"Only an expert can make sense of this"

The challenge does not reside in the accessibility of measurement data but may instead center on a lack of focus or understanding. These days, easy access to web analytics tools poses no problems. Further, reliability of the data that they provide is at its peak and available tool's ease of use should no longer form a barrier. Rather, the perspective that the above statements imply is that we fail to make sense of the data we have at our disposal. In other words, we fail to correlate said data directly to our organization's goals thereby rendering it useless. Having too much data can be a direct result of such misunderstandings. If you cannot link your data directly to the measured performance of an existing goal, there is no means with which to focus only on relevant data. A key aspect of web analytics is to focus in only on what matters most to your own goal performance as opposed to measuring everything simply because the data is there.

We Have Data So Now What?

Sometimes, common challenges associated with web analytics can be expressed by the inability to answer a question:

"Where do I go with this data?"

"How does all of this work?"

Web analytics and its related data are meaningless unless it can be placed into the proper context. That context is likely something that you already know, even if you do not realize it at first. We undertake the process of measuring and analyzing web data as a means to understand and influence the performance of our digital property. That performance is dictated by the nature and function of our web site. Purpose and functions of web sites fall within a broad range of classifications or combinations thereof. This diversity amongst the nature and purpose of sites creates a very subjective situation in that what is important to our own site's performance is unique. Understanding this fact should at least begin the process of answering where you go with your data as it will generally define the context that we seek.

You know or can certainly find out why your organization's web site was built and what offerings it allows users to access. The web analytics process will always start here and look to convert raw data into understanding and subsequent insights that can, in turn, be converted into actions that will directly influence performance results.

Organizational Challenges

Common challenges can also be derived directly from the organization itself and work to limit or prevent ones ability to get started. A lack of staffing to handle the collection, organization and analysis of data may be present. A feeling that the current staff lacks the proper expertise to conduct the various functions or web analytics may exist. The organization may be "siloed" or exhibit a general reluctance for change. Or, the people you work for may be more comfortable operating in ignorance with too much sensitivity to the real world answers web analytics can produce.

On the surface, solutions to many of these organizational challenges may appear to be out of your reach. You may not have the power to implement sweeping changes to your current organization but you do have the power to make a difference. Web analytics does not have to encompass a massive operation in order to function as a useful tool in support of various digital business decisions. A proper focus on relevant data only that exudes qualities that are measurable, quantifiable and promote an ease of understanding will alleviate some of the resource needs. In turn, this kind of information should quickly foster a competent understanding not only of what is actually happening within the web site but how said performance relates to the wider organization and its operations. This knowledge can be applied to "break" organizational silos and better handle interactions with and opinions of those that you may be reporting too.

"Web Analytics Is Hard"

Our final topic on common challenges concerns perception and may be expressed as the following quoted statements:

"Web analytics is hard"

"Only an expert can make sense of this"

"Digital media is changing too fast"

In truth, web analytics is hard. With the advent of easy access tools, it would appear that this would not be the case. However, despite this fact, many individuals and organizations struggle because they fail to see the "why" and the "how" beyond the "what" that these tools provide. Getting to this "how" and "why" our data is showing what it is can prove difficult. Couple this with the rapid change in technology that digital media is constantly experiencing and that difficulty is multiplied further.

The easy solution is to seek out an expert that can easily make sense of the "how" and "why" and not be encumbered by the dynamism of the Internet and its related technologies. There is nothing wrong with this but looking elsewhere for help does not have to be the only recourse. Despite its many challenges and perceived complexity, web analytics can be quickly learned and eventually mastered. Besides, who better to determine those "hows" and whys" in explaining results than someone that is already familiar with the web site and the organization it supports.

What You Will Get Out of This Book

We will address many of the common challenges laid out previously in order to get you started down the road toward a meaningful web analytics process. An approach will be taken that provides a simple starting point and lead readers through a logical, step by step process. The level of understanding for each reader will be taken into account by starting with very basic fundamentals and working up to more advanced concepts.   Examples and definitions will be provided where applicable to help in clarifying major points as well.

Readers who have never seen a web traffic data report or those with more experience who may be encountering some of the challenges previously discussed can benefit. We will address different steps as they apply to different circumstances such as a newly launched site or one that has been in operation for a while. We will go over in detail, the purpose of each step and why it is important. Ultimately, we will demonstrate how all of our web analytics activities fit together as they are consolidated into the formation of an overall web strategy.

The goal of this book is to provide a blueprint of steps employed to setup an organization's web analytics process and conduct such operations in a simple and efficient manner. Despite the emergence of easy-to-use tracking tools and accessible web data, many individuals lack a clear understanding of what they should be looking at or where to start. We intend to resolve this fundamental problem and allow even the most inexperienced individual to create an effective process with which to measure their web site's activity, analyze it and develop actionable insights that can be applied to influence and improve future performance.

Chapter 1

Defining Our Objectives and Goals

Laying the foundation for the entire web analytics process

A Dynamic Process

Why Is This Important?

Our first step in getting started with web analytics is to define what the objectives of our web presence are. So why start here? Simply put, the reason is to provide clarity relative to what we should be measuring and why. Web analytics can be daunting and presents many challenges, perceived or otherwise that prevent us from getting started. The best way to alleviate this is to establish a simple starting point.

Whether your site is currently being developed or has already been completed, there was, at some point, a reason or series of reasons why it was built in the first place. So ask yourself, why was this particular venture started? What did we or the wider organization expect to get out of the launch of a new web site? Who was it meant to serve? What were the intended offerings? Hopefully asking such questions result in quick, straightforward answers. In case they do not, we will look at this in greater detail soon.

As we move forward, each subsequent step will in some way refer back to the answer of these questions as they will form our web site objectives. As will soon be made clear, starting in this fashion will have formed the fundamental basis of all of our web analytics activities. We will also have defined the context with which to view our collected data and the means with which to weed out portions of that data due to its lack of relevance to the measure of our site's performance.

The Difference Between Objectives and Goals

A common problem encountered when venturing into the world of web analytics is the terminology utilized. While many of the terms used do have universally accepted definitions, there are some that do not. To ease the process of getting started and to make better sense of the information we will be covering, definitions of terms without such universal explanation will be clearly stated relative to the material in this book. The first we will encounter is the definition of goals and objectives.

Objectives

For our purposes, objectives will be defined as the high level answers to questions such as: Why does your site exist? Why was it built? What business purpose is your site meant to accomplish? The same type of questions we posited just a moment ago. We want our objectives to be clearly defined and easy to understand and are required to tailor our answers to suite these needs. Examples can include selling products, getting more customers or improving marketing efficiency.

Goals

Goals will be defined as the next level down from our overarching objectives. Specifically, goals should be the tactics employed to achieve our previously defined objectives. As an example in how to look at this, let's take the objective of selling products. Goals needed to reach this objective might be to garner site visitors, ease navigation of the site or provide products users are willing to buy. It is also important to note that like objectives, our goals need to be clearly defined and easy to understand. In addition, these goals need to demonstrate a direct influence relative to the attainment of our objectives.

Defining Our Objectives

We uncover the objectives of our site by answering one or a series of very straightforward questions:

Why did we build it?

What did we intend to accomplish when we first decided to undertake the creation of our online presence?

What is the site's business purpose?

Who was the site intended for?

What does it offer?

What do we want site visitors to do?

Why did we include that function or content?

If you were not involved with the initial development of the web presence, then reach out to those that were and pose these questions to them. Either way, the answers should be easy to provide and look something like the following:

Sell products

Obtain new customers

Market our business

Entertain users

Support our field sales team

Distribute our content and grow readership

Drive traffic to our brick and mortar locations

As we already mentioned, our intent is to place emphasis on what the site was created to do in the first place. We start with general objectives like the examples listed above and write them down. Also, you may have noticed that the questions employed to define our objectives always started with "what", "who" or "why". Your primary objectives relative to your web presence will always be an answer to a question beginning with one of these words. Once we have performed this step and documented the results, we will have established the direction of our web analytics process on a high level. Next, we move to add more detailed aspects for each be defining the goals needed to achieve them.

Defining Our Goals

Let us return again to the primary objective of selling products. If your site is focused on this, a goal example could be selling as much of product x, y and z as possible. To keep our efforts organized, under the header "Objective A: sell products", we would write down the specific goals of selling as much of product x, product y and product z as possible. You may have a pre-determined sales level to target for each and it would be appropriate to include that level of detail here.

What if the objective is to get more clients? This objective can be listed as a header (Objective B: get more clients) with more detailed signup methods listed below. Goal 1 might be to gather completed user registration forms. Goal 2 might be to garner direct inquiry emails from site visitors. Goal 3 could be to accumulate email addresses from user downloads of an online brochure.

Sometimes, a web site's objectives do not lend themselves to defining such clear cut goals. For example, if your objective is to provide useful and engaging content, more thought might be needed to determine that next level of focus. We began with an objective but now need to ask ourselves how is it intended to be accomplished across our web site and where might this occur?

To clarify, let's look at some examples of the type of questions we should be asking:

How do users buy products on our site?

Where do users buy products on our site?

How and where do we accumulate new client information?

How might users engage with our web site's content?

Where do visitors interact with our site's tools and other functionality?

We can break down the "how" further by subdividing into two distinct groups:

User actions

User engagement

Actions can viewed as a direct act that a user may perform on your site; clicking on a link, filling out a form, sending an email or buying an actual product. Engagement can be viewed as a more indirect activity. Visiting the site on a repeat basis, spending time on a specific page or viewing multiple pages within a single visit are some examples. Apply these two subcategories when thinking about how a particular objective might be reached. Your defined goals may include either direct user actions or more indirect activities depending on the nature of the objectives defined earlier. The "where" will often prove to be more obvious and simply represents the location on your site where user action or engagement can occur. If this is not the case, we will make a provision to address the "where" later on in the process.

When performing this exercise, we are trying to emulate the options provided to a typical user when visiting your site. There will be clear, direct actions that they can perform that will be easy to identify. Furthermore, there will be more general, ambiguous acts that a user can participate in like reading an article but even these can be a contributing "how" to our overall objectives. Be open to all potential options when defining your goals with an eye towards being as complete as possible. Understand that objectives sharing similar goals will be common and that it is best to include everything that you come up with at this stage so nothing is overlooked.

To summarize, the purpose of this exercise is to provide a simple means to define what our web site was intended to do and the details as to how it was meant to go about doing it. Overarching objectives are the what, who or why. Supporting goals are the how and where, whether they are defined through specific user actions or a type of user engagement. By writing them down in this fashion, we are provided with a basic overview detailing the components that define the purpose of our site.

The resulting list of objectives and related goals will differ from site to site and demonstrate a level of variety consistent with the degree of disparity inherent with the variable range of web sites and their own unique nature and functions. Because of this, there are many potential objectives and correlating goals that prove too cumbersome and to some degree, impossible to list completely. However, a list of examples covering a wider range of potential site objectives and goals can be found in Appendix A. It is by no means a complete list and is intended to support and expand upon the examples and assertions made above.

Getting Traffic, the Universal Goal

Before we move on to the next step in our process, it is important to touch on the most common goal defined in the steps above: getting more traffic. Regardless of the nature or function of your web site, getting more traffic will inevitably be listed under most, if not all of your defined objectives. So why bring this up here? Getting more traffic will always be the foremost goal of any site. It is the "how" that can be employed to achieve nearly any objective. More traffic translates to more visitors to buy products, more users to complete forms or more eyeballs for your web site's content.

However, it is important to note that high traffic, on its own, does not automatically translate into successful web site performance. If you have already listed out your own objectives and detailed actual goals for each, review them again to see how prominent "getting more traffic" is within your overview. While there is nothing wrong with listing this as a goal, we want to be sure that it is not the only goal.

We can always assume that traffic to the site and to its individual pages and sections will be tracked through our web analytics process. But, before moving forward, ask yourself this: Why do I need more traffic? In essence, view more traffic not as a goal but more as an objective. Yes, we will always want more traffic but why? Review your results from the previous steps and ask yourself this very question. Defining objectives and goals is, as already mentioned, a critically important step. Employing this last recommendation may possibly uncover key goals that you may have overlooked. Traffic is essential and will be measured, but our true need is to dig deeper in order to lay the groundwork for a more effective web analytics process moving forward.

Internal Stakeholders and the Wider Organization

So far, we have outlined the use of asking simple questions to assist in the efforts to define the various objectives and goals of your site. If you are the sole proprietor of the web property in question, this will prove adequate in your drive to define and document them. However, many readers may be entering the world of web analytics focused on a web site representing a larger organizational structure. Subsequently, there may be one or more departments or teams within that organization that have a direct interest or influence on the performance of the site.

These groups can range across many typical organizational functions and operations including but not exclusive to:

Sales

Marketing

Accounting/Finance

Legal

I.T.

These may comprise a group of internal stakeholders whose own operations and responsibilities may overlap or be directly impacted by the performance of the web site. When formulating your list of objectives and their related goals, it would be wise to reach out to these stakeholders for additional insight into the "what" and "why" of the web site's origin. Reaching out can also serve to confirm those objectives and goals you defined or to refine them to better reflect those of the wider organization.

In the introduction, organizational challenges were discussed as a common issue related to web analytics and as a potential barrier to getting started. By encouraging the involvement of other, internal stakeholders this early in the process, a large step toward eliminating those challenges can be taken. Further down the line, it is probable that their involvement will be needed again as will be demonstrated in some later steps of the process. So be sure not to overlook internal stakeholders and the wider organization as a resource as you move to complete the objective and goal definition step.

A Dynamic Process

Defining objectives and goals of your site will prove to be a rather dynamic activity. While we strive to be as complete as possible in this initial step, we may see a need to adjust our original documentation as we move deeper into the process. Later steps may weed out previously defined objectives as inaccurate or shed new light that reduces their perceived importance. In addition, moving deeper into the web analytics process may uncover entirely new objectives or goals that were not documented earlier. Regardless, it is important to view your initial overview of web site objectives and goals as a dynamic document that will experience a need for review and adjustment as we move forward. The Internet itself is a highly dynamic medium requiring flexibility in many areas in order to respond to the constant flow of changes in technologies and shifts in user behaviors. As you will see, the definition of your site's objectives and goals along with the entire web analytics process are no different.

Summary Outline

Why Is This Important?

- Defining objectives offers a simple place to begin
- Answer simple questions as to why the web site was built in the first place
- This step lays the foundation for the entire web analytics process to follow

The Difference Between Objectives and Goals

- Clearly establish the distinction between the two and their role in this book
- Objectives answer the what, for whom and why our site was built
- Goals answer how we intend to achieve those objectives on the site and where they might occur.
- It is important that both are clearly defined and easy to understand.

Defining Objectives

- Uncover objectives by answering a series of simple, straightforward questions starting with What, Who or Why
- Meant to reflect the reasons why the site was originally built
- Establish high level direction of the site based on its original intent

Defining Goals

- Defines the details describing how and where the various objectives get accomplished
- Break down the "how" into two sub categories, action and engagement

- Actions reflect more direct user activities, engagement represents more indirect activities
- See appendix A for an extended list of examples

Getting Traffic, the Universal Goal

- Traffic can be argued as a goal of nearly any objective
- It is important but does not always achieve an objective on its own
- Ask yourself why you need more traffic to clarify objective goals and ensure nothing is overlooked

Internal Stakeholders and the Wider Organization

- Internal Stakeholders are comprised of other departments or teams within an organization who exhibit a direct interest or influence on the performance of the web site
- They represent another resource with which to confirm our own assertions or expand upon them in an effort to align with goals of the wider organization
- Offers an opportunity to alleviate potential organizational challenges that may have hindered getting started in web analytics in the past
- Internal stakeholders will prove to be an important resource later in the process

A Dynamic Process

- Defining objectives and goals represents a dynamic process
- The need to adjust or add new objectives may occur as we move forward
- Important to view the objective/goal document and all of web analytics as dynamic

Recommended Exercises:

1. Document list of defined web site objectives

2. For each objective, define and document related goals pertaining to each

Chapter 2

Defining Common Metrics

Common metric definitions and the role they play in our web analytics process

Landing Page

Exit Page

Traffic Sources

Direct, Search Engine, Referral Site

Conversion Rate

Retention Rate

Key Performance Indicators

Audience Metrics

Dimension, Segment

Additional Metric Considerations

Revisiting Audience Metrics

Geography

Special Indicators

Advanced Metrics

Defining Common Metrics

In order to help facilitate your identification of metrics to employ in the measurement of your newly defined objectives and goals, we will cover the most common metrics used in tracking site performance. In addition to standard definitions, we will provide some extra insight into how or where they may fit into the overall web analytics measurement process. For more detail, it is recommended that you refer to the Google Analytics data tracking tool. It offers a great series of tutorials that not only cover the tool's function and use but also the common metrics employed and their role in various rate calculations. Use the following link to see for yourself: http://www.google.com/intl/en/analytics/iq.html

(Pay special attention to the "Interpreting Reports" section for metric details.)

It is likely that other free data tracking tools offer similar tutorials and can equally provide greater detail if you feel the need to explore this further.

Pageviews

Occurs after the loading of each independent webpage. If a visitor went from your homepage to "About Us" to "Contact Information" that would be three pageviews. Pageviews are the primary traffic measurement both for a web site and its individual pages. They are also used often in calculating other common metrics such as pages per visit, etc.

Unique Visitors

One unique, separate visitor to your site. It does not matter how many "visits" that a particular visitor has, it is still counted as one unique visitor.

Unique visitors literally measure the number of actual people who have visited your site. Like pageviews, this metric can also be employed as a common web site and page traffic measure. More importantly, it is the metric to use in calculating or counting conversions relative to specific user actions and engagement activities. The unique visitor metric serves as the most understandable measurement to convey to others when communicating web site performance results.

Visits

Defined as a single session on your web site. One visit will often contain multiple pageviews. If one visitor (user) comes to your site three times during the day, you will have three resulting visits.

Visits are useful in determining the "stickiness" of a web site. This is characterized by a user viewing multiple pages over the course of a single session. It indicates that said user interacted with multiple content areas or functions. This also may imply that your web site met multiple information or functionality needs of the visitor.

New Visits

A single session on the site by a unique user who has NEVER been to your site before.

New Visits can be used in conjunction with standard visits and pageviews to determine audience growth rate. In contrast, a simple ratio of new visits to standard visits could provide insight into the growth of repeat visitors from month to month. This metric also proves key in the calculation of the retention rate of your web site. A metric that will be defined in its own right soon.

Clicks

One is counted when a user "clicks" on an ad or link within the web site.

Tracking clicks is central to the measurement efforts of web sites focused on generating revenue from banner ad space and for affiliate marketing sites. Clicks are also useful in monitoring traffic driven to another site in that they can be compared to the destination site numbers for confirmation purposes.

This metric represents the original measurement for determining user engagement though more advanced metrics serving this purpose do exist today.

Bounce Rate

The percentage of single-pageview visits across the entire web site or an individual page. Such an occurrence is counted when a visitor leaves your site after seeing only a single page.

This is important as it may indicate the user did not find what they were looking for. It can also be viewed as a user misinterpreting the search result description or clicking on a link by accident. The bounce rate metric will serve more as a means of support later as we analyze results as opposed to acting as a direct measurement of a particular web site objective.

Pages Per Visit

Reflected by a simple calculation determining the average number of pageviews that occur during a standard visit to the web site.

pageviews / visits = pages per visit

This metric is used to measure web site "stickiness" similar to what we discussed under the visits metric. It also represents a potential measure of user engagement (indirect activity) in support of certain web site objectives and goals.

The same calculation can be performed using new visits depending on the focus of your measurement needs.

Average Time Spent

Indicates the amount of time spent on a page (average time spent per page) or on the web site (average time spent on site) during a typical user visit.

Shown in number of minutes, this too is a strong indicator of the "stickiness" of a particular web property. Longer average times translate to greater engagement with the web site's content and provide an indication to its appeal and usefulness to the user. Also, web sites focused on monetization through advertising can use this as a means to amplify the attractiveness of their site to potential clients.

Landing Page

The first page of a visit (session).

This usually will apply to your home/welcome/main page but paying attention to other common landing pages within your site can provide valuable insight into how users are utilizing it and what they are looking for prior to arriving. Identifying common landing pages also proves useful in the design and assessment of various media campaigns implemented to drive more traffic to the site.

The landing page does not represent a metric in the traditional sense but its monitoring can play a role in our web analytics process.

Exit Page

The last page of a visit (session).

Ideally, the most common exit pages within your site will reside at the end of the navigation flow existing within your site. Pages appearing after form completion or email submission also should be common exit pages.

Like the landing page, exit page identification provides greater insight into how users are interacting with your web site. Coupled with other data, it can also serve in the assessment of content and function effectiveness and user appeal. It too, does not represent a metric in the traditional sense but is worthy of attention.

Traffic Sources

Describe the means with which a particular set of users reached your web site. Data tracking tools express this count in the form of pageviews derived from a particular traffic source or the number of actual unique visitors arriving by that means. This metric is further subdivided into distinct categories and can be added to existing tracking data in support of our more primary, traffic data concerns. Reference to traffic source data will be recommended later in our web analytics process regardless of direct ties to web site objectives and goals.

Direct Traffic

Visitors who arrive on your site by typing in the URL directly (typing "http://www.gograybox.com" into their web browser).

Search Traffic

Visitors who arrive on your site via a search engine. This is both organic (non-paid) and paid search listings (PPC/SEM). It is typically subdivided by the major search engines (Google, Yahoo, Bing, AOL, etc).

Referring Sites

These visitors arrive on your site via a link from another, non-search engine site. This could be a blog post, news article, directory listing, etc. Tracking this proves very useful if you are employing various social media techniques to drive traffic to your site. In addition, identifying traffic from specific articles can provide   insight into potential best practices when creating them as well.

Conversion

Represents the completion of a specific action or activity within a web site. The "converting" action will be defined directly by those direct and indirect activities detailed within the web site's own specific goals.

Conversion Rate

Calculated as your percentage of visits or unique visitors who complete a certain, configurable goal. They are meant to express a ratio of a particular activity against the overall traffic of the web site or an individual page. This ratio differs from conversions only by its expression as a percentage rate and can be articulated in straight number counts based on the number of unique visitors who performed the action in question.

This will prove to be one of the most important metrics as we move deeper into the web analytics process. Measuring conversions against our pre-determined objectives and goals utilizes combinations of the common metrics we listed above and can serve as our primary means in measuring our site's effectiveness.

We will discuss the role and calculation of conversion rates in much greater depth later. Some common conversion rate examples include the following:

> # of emails submitted / Total unique visitors

> # of phone calls received / Total unique visitors

> # of downloads / Total unique visitors

> Total clicks / Total ad impressions

Total product sales / Total pageviews

# of completed registration forms / Total pageviews

Retention Rate

Calculated as a percentage of your visits that represent a return to your web site over the course of the reporting period being reviewed. Retention rate is expressed as a ratio of the number of return visits against the total visits that occurred and indicates the rate which users are tending to return to the web site.

Repeat visits are not commonly represented directly by their own metric but can be "backed in" using the following simple calculation:

Visits - New visits = Repeat visits

In turn, a retention rate is then calculated as follows:

Repeat visits / Total visits = Retention rate

This calculation will be employed as a measure to gauge more indirect, engagement activities. Like previously discussed metrics, it provides useful insight into web site "stickiness" and can function in direct support of the measurement of a site objective or goal.

Key Performance Indicator (KPI)

A key performance indicator (KPI) is a metric that helps you understand how you are doing against your objectives and goals.

Many of the metrics covered in this section can do the same thing and act as key performance indicators themselves. It is important to understand that the term KPI, does not represent a distinct metric measuring a single type of activity. Instead it serves as a classification used to describe only those performance metrics, which ever they may be, that stand out as the most important relative to the measurement of a specific web site's performance.

This special "class" of metrics will be discussed in great detail in a later chapter and their fundamental importance will be demonstrated in the most direct of terms soon.

Audience Metrics

Defined simply as the aggregate of users visiting your web property, an audience can be further sub-divided into a distinct segment of users displaying one or more pre-defined dimensions.

Dimension

A dimension is, typically, an attribute of a Visitor to your website. Examples include the source that someone came from (referring urls, campaigns, countries etc), technical information like browsers or mobile phones or the activity a user performed such as the pages/videos they viewed or products they purchased.

Segment

A segment consists of a group of users demonstrating one or more dimensions. Often, the best way to discover insights is to segment data using one or more dimensions (i.e. the # of Visits from, Google, Bing and Yahoo as a % of Total Visits). You segment by dimensions and report performance through the resulting metrics.

Additional Metric Considerations

Before completing our review of the common metric definitions and their role in the web analytics process, we will expand upon a few that demand additional attention. The specific objectives and goals of your site will dictate the relevance of these additional considerations to your own metric needs. However, their potential impact within the step concerning data source identification warrants at least a cursory review.

Revisiting Audience Metrics

We previously distinguished audience metrics as the aggregate of users visiting your web site which can be further sub-divided into distinct segments of users displaying one or more dimensions. The ability to break down an audience into more specific segments through data will depend on what dimensions are available through your data tracking service or other sources. Larger organizations often have the means to access this kind of data through advanced data source tools and special tag tracking of users and content areas across their site. In turn, the access to such "abilities" can represent a significant investment in staff, advanced tools and related expenses.

We are focusing primarily on getting started and will encourage ways to garner insights on our audience through more readily available options. However, even the simplest of site tracking services do offer some dimensions with which to segment an audience. Despite this, we may need to supplement our existing options by creating our own dimensions and reflecting them within our goal measurements.

To illustrate what is meant here, let's use a recruiting organization site as an example. Within their objectives and goals, the conversion of users into clients and candidates stands as a primary indicator of web site performance. The ability to segment their audience by these dimensions cannot be performed directly through the data. Instead, they segment their audience based on the pages visited within the site. They are assisted by the fact that their sub pages are organized strictly around content intended only for each of these distinctive groups. A user visiting a "client" content page can be reasonably segmented as a potential client. In the same way, a segment of "candidates" can be created. This example demonstrates that it is possible to look beyond standard or limited ranges of audience dimensions in order to segment our audience without committing to a larger investment in data resources.

Geography

Geography is used in web analytics as a common audience dimension derived from the geographic location where a specific user resides. This is often included as a tracking option within the various data tracking tools you may identify for use in your measurement efforts. However, this geographical audience dimension is commonly limited only too high level regional distinctions and may not provide the level of detail your own segmenting efforts may require.

Again, we are confronted with a situation that can be resolved through the investment in more advanced data tracking tools and tag implementations. Like in our last discussion, we can offer a simpler and less-expensive alternative as a means to continue our progress in getting started with web analytics. Web sites that are designed to serve only a local user base such as one confined to a single city or metro area will likely provide content that reflects this intended, limited focus. Similar to the example described in the last section, we can segment our local audience based on their interaction or visitation to pages offering content with only local appeal or usage. Lower geography dimensions such as metro area suburbs or zip codes may be reached by using this methodology.

The nature and purpose of your site, as always, will dictate the degree to which you may need such geographic audience segmentation to effectively measure performance. A cost/benefit analysis may be warranted or seeking a more simplistic solution like the one just described can be had rather than experiencing a hold up to the process

Special Indicators

Within the definition of conversion rates, we encountered the use of special indicators like the number of phone calls to calculate a web site's conversion rate. The term "special indicator" is not one that is necessarily used outside of this book and will be discussed briefly for the sake of clarity.

We reserve this classification for metrics that are not counted through the traditional, web traffic measurements. Often, they require a third party service or a simple manual count depending on their nature. Examples that we may encounter later (and already previously mentioned) include phone calls received by a site specific 800 number or the number of emails submitted through the site contact us page. Both of these examples have options allowing for automated or third party source tracking but it is possible that you currently do not have access to such services. While we always should seek data sources that are reliable and performed in an automated fashion, we do not want to ignore potentially key aspects of our site's activity in spite of this. You may also notice that these, special indicators as we call them, typically refer to metrics that can be tracked via a manual count.

As we move to the next step in the web analytics process, we want to take note of the use of metrics like these. It may be that the effort to collect a needed data point outweighs the value of the insights we garner from its measurement and analysis. In addition, we should be cognizant of the costs associated with accessing the needed data. If a simple, manual count can be performed in a reasonable manner, it may make sense to follow this practice versus taking on the added expense of automating our data collection needs. In other words, a cost/benefit analysis may deem the manual count to be more appropriate. However, the notion that your tracking is a manual exercise should be documented as the very nature of it implies the potential for error and a cause to question its reliability. Again, this by no means should rule out the data's usefulness, but should be noted as a potential cause in discrepancies as we later conduct our measurement and analysis steps.

Advanced Metrics

Those readers possessing more experience in web analytics and its related measurements may have noted the exclusion of metrics that, they themselves, consider being quite common. This possibility is one that is recognized and will now be addressed. Our intent is to form a strong foundation through the definition of only the most common metrics to facilitate understanding in those that are only just getting started. Those readers with some pre-existing knowledge may also derive benefit but our scope dictates coverage of the terms already discussed.

Regardless, it may be that more advanced metrics that we failed to discuss are truly just derivatives of the more common metrics but expressed in the form of more unique and varying conversion calculations. That being said, we can touch on some terms that correlate to the operation of e-commerce web sites and those focused on generating revenue through ad sales. Please recognize that the use of "advanced" as the heading of this section does not necessarily imply more difficult terms to grasp. In fact, you will see that this is quite the opposite. Instead, we view this as addressing metrics related to web site operations that offer more complexity in and of themselves and likely require expansion upon the metrics described so far. Despite our assertion that this particular topic may stray from our primary intentions, we will reference usage of some of the following terms in later sections.

Per Visit Value (E-Commerce): Average per-visit value is the average value of a visit to the site and is calculated as Revenue divided by Visits.

RPC (E-Commerce): Revenue-per-click

Average Value (E-Commerce): The average value of an e-commerce transaction.

Shipping (E-Commerce): The cost of shipping for a transaction.
Tax (E-Commerce): The amount of tax applied to a transaction. This value should be a number without any monetary symbols or commas in the value.
Transactions (E-Commerce): The total number of transactions.
Impressions (Advertising): A display of a referral link or advertisement on a web page. This metric accounts for the total number of impressions for a campaign.

CTR (Advertising): Click-through-rate is the percentage of impressions that resulted in a click.

CPC (Advertising): Cost-per-click is the average cost you paid for each click on your search ad(s).

CPM (Advertising): This stands for cost-per-thousand impressions. A CPM pricing model means advertisers pay for impressions received.

Summary Outline

Defining Common Metrics

- A quick review of common metrics employed in web analytics including pageviews, unique visitors, visits, average time spent, etc.
- Focuses on the most likely to be employed by a beginner to web analytics.
- Additional comments provided to shed light on each metric's role in web analytics
- Conversion rate and key performance indicator are briefly defined but will be expanded upon in later sections.

Additional Metric Considerations

- Site specific objectives and goals will dictate the relevance of these additional considerations

Revisiting Audience Metrics

- Available audience dimension/segmentation metrics may be limited
- Dimensions and segments unique to your site's audience can be separated based on their measured interaction or visitation of distinct content areas

Geography

- Geography tracking is often limited to high level regional designations only across the various tracking services you might be employing
- Content visitation measurement offers a potential alternative to more advanced and likely expensive geographic tracking options

Special Indicators

- Special indicators are classified as data counts that are derived from typical traffic data such as phone calls or emails
- Cost/Benefit analysis may justify their reliance versus other, more automated options

- Always note the use of manually derived data for their potential to explain discrepancies later

Advanced Traffic Metrics

- "Missing" metric definitions may be attributed to their nature as more unique conversion calculations
- The use of "advanced" in the heading refers to the more complex site functions covered rather than the terms themselves.
- Defines metrics often employed in the performance measurement of E-commerce and advertising web sites.

Recommended Exercises:

1. Perform initial assignment of metrics to serve as performance measures of your web site's documented objectives and goals.

Chapter 3

Social Media Metrics

Defining unique metrics and clarifying role in the web analytics process

Is Social Media Handled Differently?

Category Overview

General Social Media Metrics

> Return Visits
>
> Interaction Rate
>
> Video Installs
>
> Cost Per Action

Engagement Metrics

> Comments

Unique commenters

Thread size

Time with Content

Content Downloads

Subscriptions

Content Sharing

Suggestions/Feedback/Comments

Spinoff Content

Recommendations

The Value of Engagement Metrics

Social Media Application Metrics

Installs - Applications

Active Users

Audience Profile

Unique User Reach

Growth

Influence

Application Installs - User

Active users in the wild

Longevity/Lifecycle

Advanced Social Media Metrics

Is Social Media Handled Differently?

We would be remiss without mentioning social media at least to some degree as we move through the formation and application of the web analytics process. Its role has increased significantly in the last few years and is worthy of mention, even when viewing web analytics from a more basic light. Social media's role in your own web analytics process may vary but its broad influence and unique measurement metrics require some discussion before we move forward.

This may lead us to ask if social media and its related metrics are treated differently from the more common and traditional web traffic metrics discussed in the last chapter. For our purposes here, the answer is a resounding no. While social media represents a large and distinctive category within digital media, this fact does not require any major deviation from the process that we have begun up to this point or later. As will soon be demonstrated, this category does share many of the common metrics already described. Although it does expand upon them through application of a more unique set of performance measurements, their differentiation will not dictate any special treatment.

So why call such attention to social media in lieu of this stated fact? From the beginning we set out to provide a means to ease entry into the web analytics process and to mitigate any challenges that stand in the way of this. We further seek as complete an overview as possible to address the wide array of web sites, organizations and differing objectives and goals. As we mentioned a moment ago, the role social media metrics play in your own process will vary but better understanding of this topic will prove valuable.

Category Overview

The social media category has not been completely ignored throughout our previous discussions. At least one of its primary "member types", blogs, has been briefly referenced. Defined as a site used to publish opinions and commentary on various topics, its employment is widespread and may describe the web site you are looking to measure.

In addition to blogs, the social media category is also made up of more direct social media network pages such as those found on Facebook. These too, are measured through a series of unique metrics that will be defined shortly. Rounding out the category, we will take a brief look at the various web applications that provide a means for users to share information with their peers. Examples of these might include mobile and tablet applications. Neither of these later "types" represents a true web site but their potential use as traffic drivers or supplements to your own web site will compel their inclusion.

In reality, any member of the social media category may only represent a portion of the content or functionality currently being offered by your web site. The need for their measurement may have already been called to attention as goals supporting one or more of your site's objectives. With this in mind, we may now review the various metrics applicable to this category and take the opportunity to review our documented objectives and goals for more proper insertion of social media related performance measurements.

General Social Media Metrics

We earlier alluded to the fact that some of the more common web traffic metrics do apply to web sites classified within the social media category. Some of these metrics that "cross over" include:

> Unique visitors
>
> Pageviews
>
> Visits
>
> Time Spent

Their definition relative to social media remains identical as does their potential role within the web analytics process. Blogs and other social media "types" employ them to measure user actions and other activities in the same manner as previously described. However, a few derivatives that employ these common metrics that are unique to social media will be defined here.

Return Visits

Indicates the average number of times a user returns to a web site or application over a specific time period.

This is not unlike the retention rate definition mentioned earlier. Its inclusion here is meant to call out the fact that it serves as a common measure not only for blogs but for applications providing sharing and other functionality.

Interaction Rate

Represents the proportion of users who interact with an ad or application. Some will be involuntary depending on where the ad or application is placed on screen, so it is highly dependent on placement.

Note the direct correlation within our previous definition of clicks. Their employment to calculate interaction rate is likely and their role in web analytics is largely the same.

Video Installs

Tracks the number of Video players that have been placed by a user onto their page. Also called embed, grab or post, this metric is applied to the measurement of applications. This could certainly serve as the measurement for a primary objective of a particular web site.

Cost Per Action

Assignment of a cost per relevant action taken on behalf of users across the web site. This represents a calculated metric not unlike the conversion or retention rate and can be applied outside the social media category.

Relevant social media actions include:

> Contest/Sweeps Entries
>
> Coupons downloaded/redeemed
>
> Games played
>
> Videos viewed

Uploads (e.g. images, videos

Poll votes

Messages sent (e.g. Bulletins, Updates, Emails, Alerts)

Invites sent

News feed items posted

Comments posted

Friends reached

Topics/Forums Created

Number of Group Members or Fans

Reposts ("Shares")

Do any of these look like direct user actions or indirect user activities that could support your web site's objectives? If they have not been included, a return to your original document may be in order.

Engagement Metrics

We encountered the term engagement in earlier chapters and defined it as a representation of more indirect user activities that may occur across a web site. This term receives a great deal of attention in the context of social media measurement conversations. How we look at engagement and track the factors that drive it relative to social media can be accomplished through the combination and use of the common metrics to be detailed below. Note that some may involve more manual or "creative" means to generate actual, quantifiable results. Do not let this fact diminish their potential importance or preclude their use within your own web analytics process.

Comments

Literally, the number of comments made after users have read a particular article or blog post. It is a popular measure of the level or degree of discussion that content is generating.

The quality and value of the comments themselves represents another discussion altogether, but assessing the level of activity ignited by a post or article can be an indicator of whether users are engaged and feel compelled to respond.

Unique commenters

Not unlike the unique visitor metric, this counts the number of actual people engaging with a web site's content. The difference of course, is that we are looking only at those contributing to the dialogue generated through content engagement.

Increasing unique commenters over time can signal not just that you're reaching more users, but that your content is compelling and encouraging more people to engage.

Thread size

This pertains more to forums or communities, a type of web site that has received no specific mention thus far. On them, discussion questions, FAQs and support items are posted with the intent to generate user engagement. Forums and communities ar commonly associated with blogs as well.

Performance is measured by looking at the length and breadth of the "threaded" discussion that follows the original posting. This not only shows how invested participating users are, but whether the content and subsequent discussions are proving to be useful and impactful.

Time with Content

This metric directly correlates to time spent as detailed in the last chapter. Like that metric, it tracks the amount of time being spent on a page but goes a step further and relates to a specific content piece like a blog post or article.

Time with content shares the same role within web analytics as the more broad time spent metric. Likewise, it represents a more passive level of engagement with content.

Content Downloads

This is represented as a literal count of the number of content downloads that occur within a social media web site.

This was classified earlier as a direct action that users might undertake. It's inclusion as an engagement metric is justified by the level of interest in a particular content piece that its download implies. For our purposes, we continue to refer to such measurements as indicators of more direct user actions. However, the duality of use that emerges when placed in the context of social media is worth taking note.

Subscriptions

A count of the number of users signing up for access to a blog or newsletter. It is yet another example of a previously defined, direct action that can also serve as a measure of engagement in the context of social media.

We will continue to view it as a more direct action but will point out here that the act of subscribing does indicate engagement with content by the implied level of interest and the expanded opportunity it allows for user discussion and interaction.

Content Sharing

Tracks the instances of users' sharing of content with their peers. It can be expressed through the number of "retweets", emails or even reposting occurring on outside blogs.

Arguably another example of a direct user action, its frequent occurrence in any of the forms just described provides a window into the user's perception of the value of the web site's content.

Suggestions/Feedback/Comments

A count of user submitted suggestions or feedback pertaining to the site and its offerings without any direct affiliation to a particular piece of content.

This may serve as a goal in relation a primary objective but more often can be employed as another indicator to the level of user engagement across a site or series of pages within it. The act of submitting a suggestion or feedback implies that a user does care about the offerings within the web site.

Spinoff Content

This metric can be viewed as a sub division of the content sharing metric just described. Where it differs is that this focuses more on the number of inbound links embedded in blog posts or articles outside of the web site that serve to reference back to the original content.

Direct tracking of this particular metric may occur within a referring URL report (which will be defined in greater detail soon). Active inbound links will be represented here and can attest to a degree of engagement as the content clearly "sparked" another idea elsewhere. Of course, its impact on web site traffic as a distinct source should not be ignored either.

Recommendations

The number of recommendations or endorsements garnered in the form of comments or posts residing outside of the web site.

Posts and comments that recommend your web site to others can be a strong indicator of a user's connection and level of commitment and again provides indication of engagement. If discovery of outside "evangelists" is a focus of your digital efforts, the active measurement of this metric can assist in their location.

The Value of Engagement Metrics

By their nature, engagement metrics lend themselves more as indicators as opposed to direct measures of actual activities. The idea here is that by interacting with content or other users in a more obvious and consistent manner, a user is demonstrating a more committed interest in your web site. The relevance of this to the web analytics process is tied to your own understanding of engagement in the context of web site specific objectives and goals.

This means that the real value lies in tying any or all of the above metrics into other, more specific measurements that indicate positive progress toward specific, pre-defined goals. Some examples might include coupling comments with an increased number of email subscriptions or submissions. Or, correlating an increase in content downloads with an increase in sales leads or conversions. Regardless, all of these indicators are designed to measure and influence the likelihood that someone will pay more attention to your web site, more often. And by doing so, increase the likelihood that they will purchase a product, fill out a form or perform any other action that the site is focused on generating.

Social Media Application Metrics

The following metrics will relate directly to the performance measurement associated with the various mobile, tablet or embedded functionality that may be related to a web site. We only focus on providing simple definitions for each as their role within the web analytics process is consistent. Simply stated, they are each designed as supplementary metrics to enhance insight relative to application use and return on investment.

Installs - Applications

Total installations of application

Active Users

Total users interacting with an application over a specific time frame, usually by day/week/month. This is relevant because many applications have rapid growth but lose activity over time.

Audience Profile

User demographics from self reported profile information. Similar to audience segment and dimension metrics defined earlier.

Unique User Reach

A rate calculated as the percentage of users who have installed an application amongst the total social media or overall site audience.

Growth

A calculation that reflects the average number of users within a specific time frame.

Influence

Average number of friends among users who have installed the application. Indicates the level of sharing or influence and its impact on installation.

Application Installs - User

Number of applications installed by an individual user onto their profile page or other areas. Also called embed, grab or post.

Active users in the wild

Number of people regularly using an application at a given point in time. Regular usage represents a more subjective measurement but can be derived simply through common sense.

Longevity/Lifecycle

Average period of time for which an application remains installed by a user.

Advanced Social Media Metrics

This book is intended to serve as an introduction to the world of web analytics and to provide a gateway that will ease a reader's entry into it. The coverage of the unique metrics employed relative to social media was done with this spirit in mind. However, as in the chapter defining common web traffic metrics, we do want to address those readers who may have come into this endeavor with more familiarity and briefly call attention to other metrics that lie outside the scope of this book.

Within the context of social media, these pertain to measurements designed to enhance the understanding of blog or application performance relative to the selling of ad space. This is clearly relevant if your web site employs different aspects within the social media category to monetize itself and generate revenue as a primary objective. These metrics can be sub divided into three categories. We will forego providing detailed definitions as this will take us off our intended path. Instead, it is recommended that further investigation be undertaken elsewhere should any of the metrics listed below strike you as being relevant to your current needs.

Conversation Size

These metrics will help in the understanding of the breadth and depth of discussion happening in the "blogosphere" about specific topics. They also identify which topics consumers are currently engaged.

Number of Conversation Relevant Sites

Number of Conversation Relevant Links

Conversation Reach

Site Relevance

Conversation Density of Conversation Relevant Posts

Author Credibility

The following metrics assist in understanding the credibility of the authors contributing to the content. By looking at the length of time an author has been posting on a topic, the relevancy of the author's posts among peers and the frequency of posts, a better understanding of the impact of an advertisement on the web site is achieved.

Number of Conversation Relevant Posts on the Site

Number of Links to Conversation Relevant Posts on the Site

Earliest Post Date for Conversation Relevant Posts

Latest Post Date for Conversation Relevant Posts

Duration Between Earliest and Last Post Date for Conversation Relevant Posts

Content Freshness and Relevance

The following metrics help understand the freshness and relevance of the content on which an advertisement will appear. They clarify the impact of an advertisement across sites and their content within a media campaign.

Earliest Post Date for Conversation Relevant Posts

Latest Post Date for Conversation Relevant Posts

Mean-time Between Posts

Summary Outline

Is Social Media Handled Differently?

- Many common metrics apply to measurement in social media
- Although it offers a set of unique metrics, their handling in later steps does not differ from more traditional digital measures

Category Overview

- Social media includes blogs, social network pages and applications
- Applications can include mobile and tablet apps or refer to specific functionality within a web site

General Social Media Metrics

- Examples of "cross-over" metrics are listed
- Some new metrics derived directly from more common metrics are defined

- These do share roles that mirror their more common counterparts

Engagement Metrics

- Represent a more unique set of metrics commonly employed in measuring social media activities
- Each provides an indication of the level of engagement currently being expressed by users
- Some do correlate directly to defined user actions mentioned earlier but can also serve a dual purpose

The Value of Engagement Metrics

- These metrics lend themselves more to being indicators rather than measures of direct actions
- Their relevance is tied to one's understanding of overall web site objectives
- Real value can be derived by correlating some or all directly to a more definitive action

Social Media Application Metrics

- Briefly defines metrics used to measure performance of various applications
- Act in a more supplementary fashion to the more general social media and regular traffic measurements

Advanced Social Media Metrics

- Lists social media metrics tied more to advertising efforts relative to blogs
- This is done to encourage further investigation should their importance within your own web analytics process dictate

Recommended Exercises:

1. Review current metric assignments to see if any social media metrics should be added

Chapter 4

Collecting Our Data

Reviewing our data needs and identifying sources

The Next Step

Mapping Our Site

      Map Creation Tutorial

      Wrapping Up

Identifying Data Sources

      Primary Data Source

      Third Party Vendor Sources

      Manual Counts

      Objectives Lacking Direct Data Tracking Support

Our First Use of Cost/Benefit Analysis

Completing the Data Source Assessment Phase

The Next Step

The next step we will focus on is the collection of the data we will utilize in our web analytics process. Chances are, you will already have access to a variety of traffic data pertaining to your web presence. If not, there is a wide array of free services to choose from offering common, reliable metrics, ease of use and other support. Keep in mind, it is not our intent to review the different services available or label any source as more important than another. Instead, we seek to provide a means to review your current data options and organize them for utilization in later steps of our analytics process.

In cases where you do not have an existing data source, especially if the site is still being developed, we will provide guidance below in order to assist in identifying them.

Mapping Our Site

Before reviewing our collection of data source options, it is recommended to obtain a map of the property acting as the center of our new web analytics process. Doing so, provides an excellent means to identify key areas of the site that correlate to the objectives and goals we defined in a previous step. This will serve a dual purpose as we continue moving forward in our process development.

> 1. It is a simple way to gain familiarity with a site, especially if you did not oversee its initial development.
>
> 2. It also paints a clearer picture of how users might interact with the site's content and functions.

How you get started with mapping a site will largely depend on the situation. If you had overseen its development, you may already have a "map" of the various pages and sub pages. A document like this may have been created as a prelude to the actual construction of the web site in question. Was the site built by a third party developer? Reach out to them to see if they have any documentation of the site's basic architecture on hand. What if there is no document available that details the current structure of our site? Many times, a web site developer (internal or external) will set up your pages within a web analytics service tool as part of the initial site creation. In such a case, the resulting traffic reports will provide a list of all the active pages and can be used as a basis of creating a map of our own.

Map Creation Tutorial

Start on the main, home or welcome page and review the primary navigation bar of the web site. Whether it resides on the top or to the side, we will get a list of all the primary sub-pages/categories of the site content and functions here. Do the same if you have a list of pages from a pre-existing traffic report. In these cases, associate individual traffic lines within the report to actual pages on the site. Using Excel, Powerpoint or a piece of paper, create a chart flowing from left to right connecting the main page to each primary sub-page or category with lines or arrows. Be sure to include any additional main page links that may not reside directly within the main navigation bar. Sometimes, location detail pages, about us or contact us links will be found at the bottom of the main page. In addition, non-navigation links should be documented even if they lead off the site entirely. Examples might include links to external blogs, additional information resources or partner web sites. These additional links could be direct revenue generators or prove to be important performance indicators later in the process. If your site is focused on generating revenue from selling ad space, be sure to document the size and location of any ads that may reside on your front page. After completing the connection of the main page to the primary navigation sub pages and additional links, repeat the process for the each subsequent "level" of pages. The next level will often be represented in the menu options under each of the primary navigation sub page/category options. You will be documenting a path that can be followed using the connecting lines or arrows until a final end or exit page is reached. A visual example of how this might look is provided in exhibit 1.

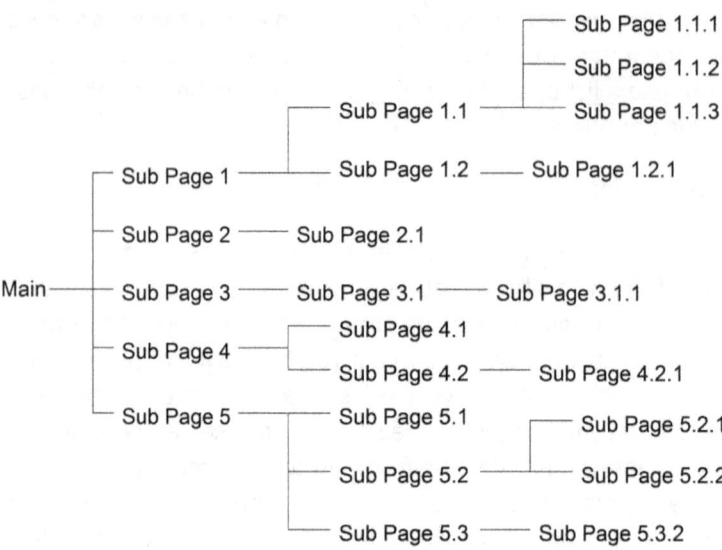

Exhibit 1: Page Map Example

We do want to be thorough in our map documentation but can sacrifice some detail if the map becomes overly cumbersome. Our intent is to allow us to gain an improved understanding of how user activity might flow through the web site and capturing every single page, especially at the lower levels can be limited if the primary goal of the exercise is reached.

Below are two additional tips to keep in mind as you endeavor to complete this exercise:

> 1. When reviewing pages or functions that request a specific user action such as completing a form, submitting a download, purchase request or email, note whether a follow up page is landed upon by the user after the action is completed. For example, a user fills out an online form and after submission; a "Thank You" page appears. Another common example; a user clicks on a buy now button. After completing the transaction, a purchase summary page is displayed. We want to be sure and include all such pages within our mapping. In later sections, they may become very important relative to our activity reporting and conversion calculations.

2. Another occurrence to look out for and document is identification of any points that lead users away from your site. In particular, you want to note these occurrences and the specific reason a user is departing. Is it to view an off-site product you wish to drive traffic too? How about a blog or community page? Maybe job listings or other information important to your organization and the site's users that are simply not currently supported within its own architecture. Again, these too, can be deemed important as we move forward in developing our process.

Wrapping Up

The end result we are looking for is an accurate layout of the site's architecture and a good understanding of where user activities take place (both direct actions and indirect engagement activities). If key functions are available across several pages, just be sure to note where for later reference. The same goes for any ad space offerings. If you have intimate knowledge of the site, this step should be quick. If not, hopefully your understanding of the site layout and functions has improved and a better understanding of how users interact with the site's operation has been achieved. You may be thinking that this represents a trivial exercise but its purpose will be made clear when we return to our completed site map for reference in later sections.

Identifying Data Sources

At the beginning of this chapter, we mentioned that there are numerous options available to serve as data sources for your web analytics process. Again, we are not looking to review and rate the various options here. Instead, we will provide a framework to assess what sources you have and which you should seek to round out your data collection needs. Ideally, all of our needed information will reside within a single data source but this is often not the case.

Primary Data Source

With this in mind, let's begin by assessing what it is that we will need to measure. Fortunately, this assessment has already been completed through our documentation of the web site's objectives and goals and initial assignment of common metrics for measurement. Each represents the most important performance aspects that we will be looking to measure. Remember, the purpose of documenting our objectives and goals was to provide the basis for a focused analytics process. The Internet allows us to measure a great deal of the activity that takes place across various web pages but we only look to focus our attention on what is important to our own performance.

Generally, every site has one primary reporting tool with which to gather its daily traffic data such as Google Analytics, Yahoo Web Analytics, Compete, etc. If you do not, I would recommend Google Analytics because of its simplicity, variety of information and price (it's free!). A quick search on the Internet will result in several free options that you can review to find the best fit for your own organization.

Third Party Vendor Sources

Daily, weekly or monthly traffic numbers derived from such standard service tools will form the basis of most, if not all of our web analytics efforts. Sometimes however, your web site may have secondary data sources that report on its user activities. Perhaps, a key objective/goal takes place on a portion of the site that is provided through or supported by a third party vendor. An example might be a career page with job listings maintained by another organization like Careerbuilder. Often, when users navigate to such a page, they are no longer tracked on your own site and have, in fact, departed to another. The user activity occurring within this off-site page is likely still critical relative to the web site's objectives and goals and needs to be accounted for.

For example, a recruiting organization with the goal of obtaining job seeking candidate signups would want to know how many occurred within their job listings maintained by a third party vendor site. They may know approximately how many visitors from their own site clicked through to the off-site page but do not have the ability to track the number that actually responded to the individual job ads on their own. In addition, the off-site career page may have had additional "candidates" arrive through sources other than the recruiting organization's web site requiring an account of their numbers. The third party vendor's own activity tracking data report would represent a secondary data source relative to the collection efforts of the original recruiting organization site.

If it is not being done so already, simply making the request to the outside vendor to supply this relevant data should suffice. This represents just one example but such arrangements, especially within the web properties of smaller organizations, can be quite common.

Manual Counts

Lastly, a third classification of data sources may need to be tapped in order to support measurement of all of the web site's objectives and goals. These can be characterized as lacking any formal report structure and emulate a more manual tracking process such as the counting of the number of emails received through a particular account (Contact Us email address) or the number of phone calls received through a site specific 800 number. Remember the reference made to special indicators in an earlier chapter?

It is possible that these examples could fall within our secondary source classification by being supported through an outside vendor's report provision but the scenarios just described do occur. In these cases, we want to note where we might obtain the information and whether it requires a manual count performed by ourselves or through another organization department or team. We also want to pay particular attention to the frequency with which said counts can change or update. Performing manual tracking operations have the potential to be time consuming and daily or even weekly counts should be avoided where possible.

Objectives Lacking Direct Data Tracking Support

What to do if, after going through each of your objectives and goals, you find that there are some that do not appear to have a data source to support them? This should be a very rare occurrence and may just be a product of not tying existing data properly to the objective and goals in question. Another review of the objective and its supporting goals might be in order. Remember, their key characteristics are that they are quantifiable and measurable and perhaps your unsupported objective does not meet these criteria. Failing this, you are encouraged to investigate the actual action or engagement activity more deeply to see if an alternative indicator (even an indirect or estimated one) exists that can be supported by your existing data reporting or manual counts. For example, the traffic from an exit page similar to those referenced earlier in the metric definition and sit mapping sections cold be used as a measure of conversion. This is done based on an assumption that a user's arrival on the page can only occur after completion of a previous action like submitting an email, or downloading a brochure.

The subjectivity of such a scenario precludes us from providing a large array of specific examples but you may have one other alternative to resolve this issue. The addition of a new tracking tag within the page or pages supporting the activity we wish to measure can be pursued. This does venture into a more advanced topic than the scope of this book is meant to cover and may be beyond your own or your organization's capabilities to implement. It is recommended that the tracking issue in question be presented to a member of the organization's I.T. team, the web site's third party developer or shopped to various tech shops to reach a viable, and preferably, cost-effective solution.

One final note on this topic concerns the accuracy of the resulting data if more "creative" means have been employed. Utilizing an estimate or backing into a measurement result by employing more indirect indicators may be the only option. You can remain confident in the reliability of data derived from your primary and secondary sources or from new tag implementation but should clearly label results data derived as estimates or indirect indicators. Not to say they do not present a useful level of insight into performance but their debatable accuracy should remain top-of-mind as we move into later steps in our web analytics process.

Our First Use of Cost/Benefit Analysis

In general, the collection of data that is employed in web analytics will prove to be a straightforward process. This is not always the case but we did address other options and circumstances that can fill any existing gaps. With this accomplished, there is one more key point to touch on before moving forward.

In today's Internet data environment, much of the needed information on web site traffic and performance measurements is provided through free service tools. Many third party vendors provide supporting data reports as part of their site, page or application support services. However, it is possible that a cost can be attached to some of the data sources you deemed necessary in this latest step. Generating such expense may be unavoidable but it is encouraged that a cost-benefit review be undertaken before making any commitments. To assist, weigh the proposed cost against benefits of the data being obtained by reviewing the factors listed below:

> Data processing time being saved
>
> Importance of the objective or goal being supported compared to others
>
> Ease with which to replace this data source with a manual solution
>
> Level of accuracy provided by the new data source
>
> The number of objectives the new data can support

Comparing cost and benefits will be a common theme as we continue down the path of building our web analytics process. Be prepared to forego the use of more accurate and detailed reporting if the resulting benefits cannot justify the expense.

Completing the Data Source Assessment Phase

With all of that said, you may have asked yourself how do you know whether a particular data source does, in fact, provide the data that you need to measure a particular objective or goal. The answer of course, lies within the actual metrics that the data source in question provides. The previous chapters on common web traffic and social media metrics can be referenced if further assistance is needed.

Summary Outline

The Next Step

- Seek a means to assess our current data resources and to identify additional ones as needed

- A detailed review of existing options will not be provided

Mapping Our Site

- A site map serves to improve understanding of the user flow across a web site
- The site map proves valuable in identifying pages where user actions and engagement take place
- A layout of the web site architecture may be provided by the actual site developer

Map Creation Tutorial

- In place of an existing site map, one can be created by following a simple exercise
- Attempt to be as complete as possible but only to the point that the general user flow and the relevant actions and activities are documented

Wrapping Up

- The intent is to gain a good understanding of the site and its functions and to identify key areas for later measurement
- The site map will play a role in later steps of the web analytics process

Identifying Data Sources

- Assess data source needs through review of the web site's documented objectives, goals and assigned metrics

Primary Data Source

- Most of our basic needs can be provided through the various free site tracking services currently available

Third Party Vendor Sources

- Reporting from secondary sources (i.e. third party service providers, partners, etc) may be relied upon if dictated by the web site's architecture and its corresponding objectives and goals

Manual Counts

- A manual counting of the number of occurrences related to specific user actions can be employed in lieu of other reporting options

Objectives Lacking Direct Data Tracking Support

- May indicate a need to review and adjust current objectives using a more quantifiable and measurable definition
- Implementation of additional tracking tags is an alternative
- "Creative" alternatives may be derived from the existing traffic data

Our First Use of Cost/Benefit Analysis

- Some needed data resources will come with an attached cost
- Conducting a cost/benefit analysis is warranted to decide whether to employ the option or seek alternatives

Completing the Data Source Assessment Phase

- A data source's relevance is determined by the metrics it provides and their own ability to meet our specific performance measurement needs

Recommended Exercises:

1. Obtain or create a web site page map

   Include all major site navigation options and sub pages

   Connect pages with lines or arrows to demonstrate potential user flow

   Include off-site links and note location of ad space

2. Identify sources that will supply results data for all of your web site's objectives, goals and their assigned metrics.

Chapter 5

Defining Key Performance Indicators (KPI's)

Emphasizing the most important metrics relative to measurement of web site performance

Using Key Performance Indicators

Control and Monitor

External Reporting

Learn and Improve

Role As A Motivator

The Most Important Metrics

The term, key performance indicator (KPI) was defined earlier as a special classification describing metrics that represent the most important measures relative to a web site's performance. Any of the common metrics that may be encountered in web analytics have the potential to be classified as a KPI depending on their ability to meet certain criteria. Further, these criteria, required to become known as a key performance indicator, will vary depending on the nature and offerings of a particular web site and its related objectives and goals.

At this stage of the process, we should already have a good idea as to which metrics will be employed to measure our own site's objectives and goals. These can be referred to as your key performance indicators from now on. However, the importance of this assignment warrants a more thorough exploration of the term key performance indicator and the characteristics that allow a metric to be classified as such.

Problems With Key Performance Indicators

In practice, the term Key Performance Indicator is too loosely defined and very much overused. For many it describes any form of data and performance metrics used to measure business performance. Instead of clearly identifying the information needs and then carefully designing the most appropriate indicators to assess performance, we often observe the following:

Identify everything that is easy to measure and count

Collect and report the data on everything that is easy to measure and count

End up getting overwhelmed with a massive amount of performance data

To avoid this common scenario, we must properly define our key performance indicators in a manner that is at the same time clear and highly relevant to our specific web site goals. We will spend some time revisiting the definition of KPI's and properly characterize them in order to ensure a thorough understanding of their nature and purpose. Also, we will continue to reference documents and findings from our previous steps as they will play an important role in identifying these crucial metrics.

Revisiting the KPI Definition

During our initial introduction, several common challenges were described that are often encountered by those new to or trying to get started in web analytics. One that stood out and that is relevant here is the fact that little or no value is being derived from the data currently at one's disposal. We reiterated this concept by citing the problem with key performance indicators as being too broadly defined and often resulting in too much data that overwhelms the analyst. We now know that a key performance indicator is a metric intended to gauge only the most important aspects of a web site's performance and emphasized the fact that we measure only the most important activities to narrow focus and avoid theses common problems.

If you have been following along and implementing each of the recommended steps, you already have created a list of key performance indicators for your web site. The opening paragraphs and sections of this chapter were dedicated to impressing upon readers the importance of key performance indicators yet no additional means to define them beyond basic definitions of common metrics has been provided. In reality, the relative importance of any particular performance metric will be derived through very subjective means. This point has been made and will continue to be referenced as an inescapable truth concerning web analytics. However, we can attempt to address this apparent gap by providing a more in depth explanation of what a key performance indicator is and use it as a means to test our earlier metric assignments and confirm their quality.

Let us begin by breaking down each component word from this term starting with "Key". A metric can be considered "Key" when it is fundamental to the success or failure of the organization and its web property. To clarify, employee turnover is considered to be an important aspect of an operation. However, it is rarely a make or break element relative to the success or failure of the organization. If you can operate below typical benchmark levels and still receive satisfactory results relative to overall organizational efforts, then the component is likely not "Key". This calls attention to our previous point that the simple ability to quantify and measure, does not automatically translate into a need to do so within a web analytics process.

Next let's look more closely at the "Performance" component of KPIs. A metric relates to organizational performance only when it can be clearly measured, quantified and easily influenced to impact results. We have already clarified that an opportunity to quantify and measure does not impact our decision to employ a metric as a key performance indicator. Instead, we look here to a metric's characteristics concerning the relative ease to influence or impact results. Each of the most common metrics offer some means of directing influence by those operating an organization's web site.

For example, web traffic metrics can be influenced through a variety of techniques like media campaign implementation or adjustments to site structure or offerings. Likewise, manipulation of traffic metrics influences results of potentially key web site activities like product sales, email submissions, and form completions. The ability to measure and quantify stand as minimum criteria relative to the measurement of any performance activity but making an argument relative to an ability to influence outcomes is the difference maker that we can draw from here.

The "Indicator" component alludes to whether a metric provides information on future performance. It can be argued that much of the data available to an organization has value only from a historical context. In web analytics, this "history" of information can be very useful and will play a significant role in later sections. However, "Indicators" should mirror exactly what is implied; they are a metric that indicates the potential future growth or decline of our web site performance. Not unlike the reference made during our review of engagement metrics and their value.

Target Values

Before moving on, there is one more aspect of the key performance indicator to clarify. Any KPI cannot be established without a clear understanding of what is possible. What we mean by this is that both the upper and lower limits of the KPI metric performance relative to the market, competition, similar organizations or our own historical results needs to be considered. Targets such as these are the elements that make key performance indicators useful in our efforts to measure the execution of our online endeavors. It is likely that our earlier efforts to identify web site objectives and goals may have already defined this needed target range. If not, use this opportunity to review your current list and add this detail if possible (sources for benchmark data and development techniques will be addressed in a later chapter). The absence of such benchmarks may indicate that your selected goals and their related metrics may not meet the more stringent criteria stipulated by our new, more expansive definition of key performance indicators.

Designing and Selecting Key Performance Indicators

Let's take a step back and inspect our expanded view of how a key performance indicator is defined. First, these metrics include the following criteria:

> Quantifiable and measurable
>
> Correlate directly to key web site objectives and goals
>
> Offer an ability to influence results
>
> Indicate potential future performance
>
> Have benchmarks to define performance limits

Furthermore, key performance indicators are meant to do the following:

> Narrow focus and limit the amount of data we are working with
>
> Improve our ability to derive valuable insights

Their service as a direct manifestation of web site goals and the foundation of our web analytics process supports the assertion that a high degree of attention be paid to their design and selection. If you have been performing the exercises recommended thus far, you will have a list of metrics, now labeled as key performance indicators that require a return visit to ensure their placement within this important classification. To assist with this effort, we will turn our attention away from general definitions and look more to the details behind their choosing.

The Question Is The Answer

A good place to start is to return to the questions asked of yourself or others within the organization that were meant to identify the web site's strategic objectives. Then, we asked what we are doing and for whom. We also asked why these efforts were being undertaken. Following up with these answers, we asked how do we go about accomplishing this and where those actions and activities might occur.

We can now review our initial metric assignments to measure the results of these "answers" by asking the same set of questions again but with those specific metrics in mind. Do the metrics we selected serve to answer the question being asked as clearly as before? Would another metric or combination of metrics prove to be a better fit? This exercise is repetitious but offers the most direct means with which to assess our previous choices.

Revisiting Conversions

Conversions or conversion rates represent the best choice for metrics meant to serve as key indicators of performance. This fact was alluded to earlier as they were defined amongst the most common web metrics. Why this is the case relates to the fact that these metrics quantify and measure the important outcomes that a web site was designed to generate. These outcomes, whatever they might be, form the foundation for which the web property was originally built and will further dominate the attention or intent of any business decisions made to alter or impact their performance.

Conversion rates will typically be comprised of very small percentages often not exceeding ranges of one to three percent. They drive to the very heart of why your web site exists but the value in these metrics can become even more apparent. This occurs when one considers the fact that they can also call greater attention to the remaining 97-99% that do not convert.

It can be easy to apply such conversion measurements to many of the direct actions derived from user activities occurring across the web site. They may already have been listed as the primary metric option within your list. However, we do want to offer consideration for their use in the measurement of the more indirect activities as well. Content consumption or other indirect engagement type activities may offer the potential for expression as conversions as well. Take this opportunity to reconsider this possibility as you review metric assignment as key performance indicators.

Other Factors to Consider

The design and selection of key performance indicators can be enhanced through consideration of some additional factors. We have already touched on the need for simplicity to better facilitate focus and ease of understanding. We have also pointed out the use of conversion rates and their foundation based on the measurement of key outcomes that might occur within a web site.

Multi-period Comparison: We can add to this first, by contemplating their usefulness as a comparative tool spanning multiple reporting periods. A key aspect of an effective key performance indicator is its ability to remain consistent from year to year. When settling on metrics to employ to calculate a key conversion, those used need to remain consistent on an ongoing basis. For example, will you track product sales using the dollar amount sold or the number of units? Also, will returns be factored into the monthly totals on a regular basis or not.

Moreover, usefulness over multiple periods can be assessed by a metric's ability to offer insight through multi-period comparison analysis. Do its results lend themselves only to single period performance measurement or can it be analyzed just as easily in larger increments? Consistent use of metrics can ensure this ability but it is important to note that this additional aspect has much to do with the analyzers mentality as well. When choosing your key performance metrics, be sure to account for the possibility that that this kind of analysis will be employed.

High Focus Activity: When reviewing your key performance indicator metric selections, are you leveraging measurements that correlate to areas where you are or plan to spend a good deal of effort? If done correctly, your identified objectives and goals should cover areas that will dominate your attention from period to period. Simply ask yourself if the metrics being employed reflect this same characteristic. Ideally, all of our key performance indicators will reflect a direct correlation between what we measure and where the majority of our time and attention will be placed.

Segmentation: The next consideration factor relates to a metric's ability or opportunity to segment its results. In other words, can we subdivide periodic performance results into smaller groups based on the type of user that performed the actions or activities they reflect?

This of course can also call into question the capability of your designated data source and its ability to provide such information. However, as you continue to deepen your web analytics experience and expand the level of insight needed to assess and influence your web site's performance, this factor's presence relative to your chosen KPI will increase in importance. Consider this aspect when selecting your metrics even if the need is not readily apparent.

Addressing The Customer: Any performance measurement utilized in relation to a web site will reflect user actions or activities in some form. The rise and fall of site traffic can serve as an indicator of customer interest or acceptance. Similarly, the number of purchases or downloads and the level of user engagement can provide these kind of indications.

Consider that when you are measuring performance, your intent is to increase understanding of user activity in order to make better business decisions later that can influence them in the direction you wish to move. Some, if not all of your key performance indicators should provide for this level of insight so that this influence can be achieved.

Link to Traditional Metrics: This factor is rooted in the characteristics of the wider organization that the web site represents. If your organization undertakes activities outside of the digital arena, it will have a set of "metrics" used to track that activity. The end result of these outside efforts may be exactly the same as those sought on your web site. Targeted end results like product sales or customer acquisition and retention come to mind. What we are saying here is that your selection of key performance indicators employed on the digital side of the business should share similar characteristics as those used elsewhere in the organization. By mirroring wider organization performance measurements directly with your key performance indicators, the ability to seamlessly combine and compare metric results from digital and more traditional operations is possible. This becomes especially useful in reporting performance to executive management, coordinating marketing efforts with other departments or when seeking to demonstrate web site revenue or return on investment relative to the wider organization.

Competitive Intelligence: Within the scope of this book, we view the collection of competitive data as a distinct type of measurement activity. In a later chapter, we will address this in more detail. When designing and selecting key performance indicators, competitive intelligence can prove to be a factor of consideration in two ways.

First, competitive data can be employed in the establishment of benchmarks which serve as a key component of effective KPI metrics. Second, one can consider the possibility of utilizing actual competitive data metrics as key performance indicators themselves. Consider the fact that a web site's performance can and should be compared to results obtained by similar sites or from direct competition to assess how it is doing. In this light, tracking results from outside the organization can serve as a significant indicator as to how performance should be viewed.

Access to this kind of information will vary depending on your own available resources. However, like the array of tracking services that are currently available, a similar set of competitive intelligence tools are also at your disposal and will be discussed in greater detail soon.

Brand Measurement: The final factor we will touch on here relates to the measurement of an organization's brand through the tracking of activity across its web site. Measuring the impact that digital activities have on an organization's brand is a hotly debated topic these days. It certainly warrants a much deeper discussion on its own but we will focus only on its implication in the selection or design of key performance indicators here. Different aspects of site usage can prove to function as brand lift indicators and, when coupled with direct links to wider organization metrics, can be included in these assessments that might be viewed elsewhere in the organization. Further, a web site's retention rate can be interpreted as a measure of customer loyalty providing insight into the impact on the organization's brand.

When just getting started, these kinds of considerations will likely not be top-of-mind. Brand measurement may not be reflected in your initial web site objectives and goals but should at least be considered as a potential factor when settling upon key performance indicators to be used in your web analytics process.

Using Key Performance Indicators

Key performance indicators exist to measure the performance of a web site. Further, their fundamental purpose or use in the completion of this effort can be summarized by the following:

> To control and monitor
>
> To report externally
>
> To learn and improve

Your own key performance indicators should support each of these differing aspects and we will spend some time on each next.

Control and Monitor

This use of key performance indicators calls attention again to the adage that we can only control what we can measure. This represents a founding principle of web analytics and is no less true as we explore the use of KPIs. Likewise, our effort to narrow focus and carefully select only those metrics that are the most relevant to our web site's performance also reflects this use. We look to our key performance indicators to control and monitor not only results but the direction and focus of all digital operational efforts that might be undertaken. In other words, they serve to unify the organization behind management and influence of the activities that they convey.

External Reporting

Key performance indicators are also utilized to inform other stakeholders that may have direct or indirect influence or interest in the performance of the web site. Proper selection of metrics can help facilitate better communication of the outcomes occurring online. They will also find a place within other reporting functions that tie to more traditional organization performance measurement and serve to weed out any non-digital data that is not relevant to the performance of the web site itself.

Learn and Improve

This represents a key performance indicator's most natural use. They are intended to equip the analyst with the information needed to make better, more informed business decisions that will lead to actual improvement. In this context, KPIs are used internally as the evidence to support management decisions, to challenge assumptions and to create an atmosphere of continuous learning. Further, they provide clear understanding of what indicators are required for learning and which to focus on for improvement.

KPIs As A Motivator

Once you have good key performance indicators defined, ones that can be quantified, measured and easily reflected in your web site's goals, what do you do with them? We answered that to a great degree by summarizing their different uses a moment ago. However we can expand on this a bit more as we reflect on their role as a motivator.

You use key performance indicators as a performance management tool, but also as a carrot. KPIs give everyone in the organization a clear picture of what is important and of what they need to make happen within their own roles. You use that to manage direction and to motivate the people in your organization to focus on meeting or exceeding those key performance indicators. Post the KPIs wherever they can be seen: in the break room, on conference room walls, on the company intranet, or even on the web site itself. Show what the target for each key performance indicator is and show the progress toward that target for each of them. Share them with the digital team and communicate them to other internal stakeholders. Use them to motivate others and even yourself to reach and exceed those KPI targets.

Summary Outline

The Most Important Metrics

- Moving forward, those metrics employed to measure web site objectives and goals will be referred to as key performance indicators
- Their importance is grounded in the fact they will drive all of our measurement efforts

Problems With Key Performance Indicators

- KPI represents a broad and over-used definition
- Its general nature can inspire a tendency to identify all data that is easy to collect and measure leading to an overwhelming amount of data with no clear focus
- Accentuates the need for careful design and selection of performance metrics

Revisiting the KPI Definition

- Seek a more refined definition in order to address the gap implied by viewing common metrics as KPIs
- A metric can be considered "Key" when it is fundamental to the success or failure of the organization and its web property
- A metric relates to organizational performance only when it can be clearly measured, quantified and easily influenced to impact results
- A metric serves as an indicator when it provides information on future performance
- Pre-defined benchmarks detail the range of possibilities that a KPI metric should represent

Designing and Selecting Key Performance Indicators

- Proper metric selection is based on its ability to best represent web site objectives and goals
- Can the metrics themselves serve to answer the questions posed to define goals?
- Conversions are the top choice of metrics to serve as KPIs

- Other factors to consider when selecting KPIs include: Multi-period comparison, leveraging high focus metrics, segmentation, addressing customer voice, links to traditional metrics, employment of competitive intelligence and ability to measure branding

Using Key Performance Indicators

- KPIs can be utilized to control and monitor operations, serve in external reporting and allow for learning and improvement
- KPIs can also be used to motivate and direct the team

Recommended Exercises:

1. Review existing metric assertions using the more stringent KPI definition and details

2. Design and select new key performance indicators as needed

Chapter 6

Organizing Our Data

Preparing our data to ensure efficient and effective measurement

Key Reports

General Web Traffic Reports

Page Popularity

Home Page Visitors

Bounce Rate

Referring Search Terms

Referring URLs

Page Referral

Site Overlay

Prepping Our Data

By now, we should have a clear understanding of what the goals of our web property are and what key performance metrics will make the most sense in measuring effectiveness relative to these defined user actions and activities. We will now turn our attention to a series of steps that will prepare us for the actual measurement of our web site's performance.

When we first introduced the direction of this book, we touched on the idea that a systematic approach would be taken. In addition, we emphasized the need to construct our web analytics process in a manner that would optimize efficiency. Taking this a step further, we expect this approach to result in a far more effective process that will mitigate the various challenges one might encounter when first getting started.

Our next series of discussions will center on proper organization of our data and related KPI metrics as a prelude to the actual measurement and later analysis of our collected results. Our efforts will involve a manipulation of the collected data into a form that will better gauge these results and allow for deeper analysis as we seek greater insight into our web site and its operations. The proceeding topics will ensure that our data is properly prepared and ready for use in a more effective and efficient means to measure performance.

Data Classifications

Before we get into organization of data, we want to subdivide the information we will be working with into two distinct classifications:

> Current Results Data

> Historical Data

As you can see from our labels, these two "classes" of data our differentiated based on the time period with which their results are tied. We will refer back to these two data classifications often as we move into later steps of the process. So with that in mind, let's take a look at each more closely so that this distinction is made clear.

Current Results Data

From now on, we will refer to our collection of metric (key performance indicator) results from the most recent time period as our current results data. The definition, length and implementation of reporting time periods will obviously impact exactly what set of our data qualifies as current. This will be a topic that we explore in much greater detail very soon as it has many implications relative to the organization of our data. For now, however, we simply want to establish that data from our most recent reporting period will be referred to or classified as "current".

Historical Data

Our remaining data outside of the most recent "reporting period" will be classified as historical. This label, in and of itself, offers no great revelation and is readily admitted. However, historical data plays a key role in our measurement and analysis activities and will be repeatedly referenced as we delve deeper into the web analytics process. This data will be employed in different forms to serve as our primary "measuring stick" of current results. It will serve as a catalyst in identifying areas that demand further investigation and may have already been used in the selection of the key performance indicators that will drive our efforts.

Data Quality

In previous sections, we have touched on the quality of the data we were collecting. Although, we expressed confidence in the reliability of data provided through the more common data tracking services, we did encounter potential circumstances where accuracy or reliability could be questioned. As we have already discussed, the weighing of cost and resulting benefits may have conspired to concede acceptance of certain shortfalls and we are not changing that stance here. We still suggest that notations be made relative to any such circumstance lying within your own data.

Instead, we want to point to another aspect that impacts the quality of our data; the span or depth of our historical data that we just classified. At different points throughout our later discussions, we will detail more specific uses of historical data within the web analytics process. A common theme will arise demonstrating the impact your historical information's depth will have on these future steps. Often, a greater range of supporting results from the past will offer more accuracy or reliability as we make assertions pertaining to our current performance.

The ideal situation is for you, as a newcomer to web analytics, to have access to a wealth of prior performance results going back several years or more. Unfortunately, this could very likely not be the case. We are calling attention to this now to first help form the context of later discussions. Second, we DO NOT want to view a lack of extensive historical data as a reason to forestall our efforts in getting started within a web analytics process. Moving forward, we will address situations where a web site may have just launched or is too new to have generated much, if any historical performance results.

We will provide ways to continue pushing forward despite any disadvantages relative to data access. Besides, each subsequent reporting period that you pass through will serve to enhance and increase your wealth of historical data.

Organizing Our Data

Whether we are dealing with a mountain of past performance data or just starting out with the site's first few weeks of results, it is important that we establish a consistent method to organize it for use in our web analytics efforts. We mentioned earlier that an important aspect of key performance indicators is that they can remain consistent from year to year. We need to take this concept into account when organizing our data as this will ensure a more reliable and consistent comparison over the course of subsequent years.

Establishing the Report Time Period

We start organizing our data by establishing a standard time period with which to assign or categorize results. The most common option is to break down our data into monthly "pieces". A single month provides enough time to collect a meaningful amount of data yet does not allow too much time to pass before we are able to analyze it and take any appropriate actions. However, as we first mentioned in the Data Quality section, your current circumstances may dictate otherwise. If your site has just launched, you will not have the benefit of comparing results to past performance spanning several months or more. In these cases, you certainly do not want to wait until enough time has passed to collect this much data. Instead, it would be best to subdivide your monthly reporting into single week or even daily increments. A consistent unit of time is needed to compare results and establish traffic and conversion trends and in cases like these, we still will look to establish the more common monthly reporting increments we recommended earlier. However, in the short term, this simple subdivision will suffice in lieu of access to more data over longer periods in the future.

We employ these shorter reporting periods when little or no historical data is available because we can still record and quickly review any initial trends in our activity. Ideally, our data will show nothing but growth in the first days and weeks after launch but it is possible they will not and we do not want to be inactive during this key period. Regardless, when faced with such circumstances the recommendation here is to switch to a monthly reporting period in full after about three months.

Report Compilation

With the report timing determined, we want to focus next on ensuring good organization of the data itself. In our discussion of key performance indicators and data collection, we emphasized the need to avoid capturing all of the data available and centering only on the results relevant to our own site's objective and goal measurements. If we have consistently followed the steps laid out thus far, we should have decided upon a series of KPI's and the specific metrics needed to measure them. Typically, most of these metrics will be derived from the standard traffic data tracked through our chosen primary data source. We may also have added some secondary sources and/or data requirements derived from manual counts. In any case, we want to organize the reporting of this data in line with our recently established reporting time period, most likely by month.

Most web site traffic services offer custom reporting options that you can set up within their traffic tool. Remember, these can be easily adjusted later if any additional reporting needs arise as we move into later chapters. When setting these up, you will include many of the most common traffic metrics including Pageviews, Unique Visitors, Visits, Time Spent and Bounce Rate. Secondary, manual and social media related collection options will likely not provide the degree of customization like these primary data sources but at least they can be arranged to reflect the monthly time period serving as our initial means to organize our range of data. Your end result will be either a single report or a collection of data from a series of reports encompassing a range of different sources.

Using A Single Data Source: When using only a single source of data, the reporting it generates can be used directly within our later measurement and analysis steps. Our only consideration here is to ensure that a meaningful comparison of the results from each monthly (or shorter) reporting period can be performed. This can be done by taking an additional step and transferring each monthly report to a central collection worksheet. This will promote efficiency later in the web analytics process for the ease of comparison it allows between different reporting periods. This will also have an impact on our process effectiveness as will be demonstrated in later sections.

Using Multiple Data Sources: Having multiple data sources can make this proposed "data merge" a bit more complex but the same principle can be applied. When faced with this situation, the combination of our data from these differing sources into a central worksheet takes on more importance. We still are looking to easily perform metric comparisons from period to period. Combining them into a single data set will accomplish this and set the stage for greater efficiency and effectiveness. Of course, we will need to add a few intermittent steps to get to this point but the effort will prove worthy.

First, we need to review the reports obtained from each data resource to identify consistencies that may already exist. Pre-organization according to monthly increments of time should be present. Other consistencies to look for might include the following:

> All use similar spreadsheet software like Excel

> Similar column or row orientation

> Similar period begin and end dates

> Report on the same metrics

The degree of consistency will vary and in the case of manual tracking, possibly not exist at all. Regardless, we next seek ways to manipulate each until a consistent format is achieved. To help with this process, here are a few quick tips:

Select one of your reports as the primary

It can be the one produced from your primary source or the one containing the most widely used information relative to your KPIs

Convert the others into the same spreadsheet software (Excel, etc) that is used with this primary report

Choose the most consistent row and column orientation present within your range of reports

Using this structure, combine the differing data into the central document on a per month basis

Ultimately, we want to spend our time and energy reviewing and comparing the information rather than entering it into our new, central collection spreadsheet. However, spending time developing this report now will allow for this better use of time and energy later. Excel was referenced a few times in our list of quick tips covered above. To further assist in your own efforts, a detailed example using Excel is provided below.

Creating A Central Worksheet Using Excel: First, if conversion to Excel is needed for any of the reports, be sure to leave these reports untouched, in their original state, after conversion. Next, create an Excel spreadsheet with a series of worksheets to copy and paste these newly converted reports in their original format. You can create one worksheet that acts as your central document. It then can "pull" the data from the newly pasted original reports that reside within their own worksheet tabs. The original structure of these differing reports can and should remain the same. Using basic Excel functionality, needed data results from a wide array of differing report formats can be added to the central document where more meaningful arrangement, calculation and presentation can occur. This "technique will ease the conversion process and focus your data organization more on the central document instead of each individual report contributor. Doing this will also serve to automate the merging of the data once the initial set up is complete and save a lot of process time at the end of each period. The key here is to leave the periodic reports in their original state so they remain consistent each time they are copied and pasted into your central collection spreadsheet. If you have key data that can only be manually counted and entered, just be sure to include an entry point somewhere that will include it within the periodic data compilation whether it be within its own worksheet or directly within the central collection document.

We can spend a lot of time discussing different Excel formulas and formatting techniques but will instead recommend utilizing the Help option if you need any assistance.

Document Your Compilation Process: One other tip to keep in mind when performing this exercise is to document any steps required each reporting period to complete the compilation of data. This documentation will serve to define the first steps of your regular, periodic web analytics process and can be referenced later by yourself or anyone who may be stepping in to perform these duties at a later date.

Additional Report Considerations

Before moving on, we will address one more potential data organizational issue. Our key performance indicators may require looking at various data by an individual page or pages. Reports derived from common data tracking tools will almost always provide this type of breakout as a standard option. You will likely need to look at results at this level for some, if not all of your KPI's so remain cognizant of this fact when organizing your data. Breaking out results by page will complicate the compilation process but may be warranted if your web site measurement goals dictate this inclusion. Only highlight or include those pages that are actually relevant to the overall measurement goals of the web analytics process and be sure to clearly distinguish them within your central collection spreadsheet versus the web site's overall traffic numbers.

Key Reports

In this chapter, we have focused on the basics of getting our collected data organized in preparation for more meaningful measurement and analysis. We have discussed the various reports that comprise this data but only in very general terms. In fact, we have only really touched on reports based on their relative source with little said about their actual content. Before we move on to the next major topic, we will briefly discuss examples of different reports and what they add to our web analytics process. Furthermore, their inclusion within the compilation efforts described above will be dictated by their service needed in the measurement of our key performance indicators. Such a relationship will ensure that the data they provide will be counted on for each reporting period. Those that do not dictate this level of inclusion may still prove useful as we shall see in our later measurement and analysis phases.

General Web Traffic Reports

All of our previous discussions have presumed that the reports we will be working with are comprised of data reflecting various traffic results across our web site. These general traffic reports are and will continue to be the formative backbone of our web analytics process. Their role is universal and their importance is paramount. Calling attention to this fact here serves no other purpose than to help distinguish the reports we will be describing next.

Page Popularity

In many cases, viewing the "popularity" of the individual pages within your web site will be essential. This report measures popularity simply by ranking pages according to the level of traffic they garnered. In truth, this is no different than the general traffic report described a moment ago. We mentioned traffic tracking by page as an additional consideration relative to our report compilation again because of the potential complexities inherent in any attempt to include this level of detail with our monthly data. Our KPIs may make this a moot point in either direction but this report and the insights it can provide into content interaction will warrant a look.

Home Page Visitors

This report offers yet another instance where the information it provides is likely already reflected in our general traffic data. The importance of the home page does actually vary depending on the nature and offerings of any particular site. E-commerce sites offer a good example as the range of actual visitation entering through their home pages can range from as low as 10% to a more common 50-60%. This is a direct reflection of the influence search engines and their impact on user's ability to arrive just as easily on any internal web site page. Again, this information may be included in your existing traffic reports but a separate viewing can aid in efforts to better calibrate any resources dedicated to your web site's main page.

Bounce Rate

We defined bounce rate earlier as the percentage of visitors who left your site after generating only a single pageview. This implies that said visitors did not engage with your content or other offerings before leaving. In other words, it stands as a representation of your failure rate. This report, coupled with referring URL (traffic source) data will serve as a key resource as we dive more deeply into performance results. This metric is offered in conjunction with more general traffic data and may even, in some cases, serve as a key performance indicator. Whether it is compiled with other data or not, bounce rate will be referred to again later in our process.

Referring Search Terms

This tells you which search phrases people are currently using to find your site with an option to view both in paid or unpaid terms. Obviously, this report's use will correspond directly to any search related efforts to drive traffic to your site. This of course can relate to the universal goal of driving more traffic and prove useful in optimizing your efforts for the best results. More importantly, this report can offer a window into the minds of your web site visitors by revealing what it is that they want. Each search term is a reflection of what it is that they seek and can serve to foster a better understanding of the site's user base.

Referring URLs

This report lists the web sites that are currently sending you traffic. We can expand upon this to include the referring search engines as well. This information was touched on back when we defined traffic sources as a common metric and we highlighted it as a potentially useful data set within our web analytics process. Referring URL information can also be employed as a useful audience segmentation tool relative to overall site traffic and as a means to sub divide user's performing specific web site goals. The added complexity to our monthly reporting that it could generate may preclude its regular inclusion but its value and usage will remain nonetheless.

Page Referral

This report details the relationship between the individual pages of your site in a similar fashion to the URL referral report mentioned above. Rather than looking outside your web site, it instead provides the amount of traffic referred from one page to another. How this relationship is expressed will vary depending on the tracking tool in use but the resulting report will not differ greatly from the page map we obtained back in chapter four. This report will best serve in a supporting role relative to the rest of our combined monthly data and, like many of the other reports we have discussed, could be referenced again in later phases.

Site Overlay

This report displays an actual page found within your site, just as they look to visitors but with a click level indictor beside each link. It can also provide the number of actual people (unique visitors) who click on each link. This, of course, can be repeated for any or all of your web site's active pages if need be. Used in conjunction with other data, like audience segments, one can begin to identify user "paths" that most result in sales or the completion of other goals. It also can prove a quick way to measure the success of any newly implemented links and other features. Another use can relate to testing, or rather serve as a replacement to more traditional testing methods (which we will discuss later). With your site overlay report in hand; one can visit competing sites or those supported by much larger organizations. Doing so can serve to bolster competitive insights or allow you to piggy-back on the testing larger organizations, with much greater resources, have most assuredly done. Chances are, there own link placement has already been justified by careful testing to determine the optimum placement and wording.

Summary Outline

Prepping Our Data

- Dedication to solid data organization will result in a more efficient and effective web analytics process

Data Classifications

- Sub divide our data into two distinct classifications

Current Results Data

- Represents data reflecting performance results from the most recent reporting period

Historical Data

- Represents data reflecting performance results from the remaining, previous reporting periods
- Historical data will play a key role in the coming measurement and analysis phases of the web analytics process

Data Quality

- Again reference the need to note instances where data is derived from manual, or other more "creative " means
- The "quality" of historical data is dependent on the depth of the results it includes based on how far back in time it goes

Organizing Our Data

- Organizing our data in a consistent manner is a very important aspect of our measurement efforts
- The value of our KPIs dictates the need for consistent comparison from year to year and can be ensured through organizing efforts

Establishing the Report Time Period

- We start by establishing a period of time with which to base our organizational efforts upon; preferably one month
- In the absence of any existing data, we shorten this period to a week or less until more information can be collected and the standard monthly increment can be implemented

Report Compilation

- We encourage the consolidation of information into a central reporting spreadsheet to better facilitate period to period comparison
- This becomes more necessary if multiple data sources are being employed
- Various tips and examples are provided to assist in the compilation process
- All procedures required to complete this compilation should be documented for future reference

Additional Report Considerations

- Some key performance indicators will dictate the need to track results by individual page
- Combine only those areas that are directly relevant to avoid too much complexity in the central report

Key Reports

- Provides some detail relative to some different types of reports and their usefulness

General Web Traffic Reports

- References the majority of web traffic reporting we will be working with

Page Popularity

- Breakout of traffic by individual page
- Recommended separately as a useful tool in later analysis

Home Page Visitors

- Breakout of traffic of the web site home page
- The importance and inclusion of theses results within the more standard data compilation will be dictated by the nature and offerings of the site

- Useful in managing resources dedicated to a site's main page

Bounce Rate

- Dedicated to reporting the "failure rate" of the web site and its individual pages
- Can also be included within the larger report document
- Will prove as a useful resource in later sections

Referring Search Terms

- Details the search terms used by visitors to find your site
- Corresponds directly to search related, traffic driving efforts
- Offers insight into what your users actually want

Referring URLs

- Refers to the various sources of traffic to our web site
- This information has already been identified as playing a role in later process steps

Page Referral

- Demonstrates how much traffic is referred on a page to page basis within the site
- Represents another potentially useful analysis tool

Site Overlay

- Displays a web page, exactly as it is seen by a user but with the addition of click and unique visitor counts by each link
- Provides insight into user site behavior
- Can also be employed in competitive analysis and used as an alternative to more traditional site testing

Recommended Exercises:

1. Organize data into monthly increments

2. Consolidate monthly reports into a centralized worksheet

Chapter 7

Measuring Performance

Diving into our results data setting the stage for deeper analysis

Measurement Supplement

Role of Historical Data

Establishing and Comparing to Our Base Performance Levels

Creating Value

Competitive Intelligence

Google Trends for Websites
Attention Meter
Statbrain
Compete

Quantcast
Quarkbase

When All Else Fails

Measurement

Measurement is defined as the act or process of ascertaining the extent, dimensions or quantity of something. This process is often performed through the comparison with an existing standard. Taken together, we have a description that fits nicely within the scope of the web analytics process.

First, we quantify the various actions and activities occurring across our web site through the use of a variety of data tracking resources. In addition, we identify those resulting data sets that best correlate with the most relevant behavior pertaining to site performance in the form of key performance indicators. Finally, we organized that data into a consistent format for better use in comparison as we build a results database. If you have followed each step as they have been laid out to this point, a significant portion of the measurement process has been completed.

The second part of the measurement definition highlights the need to compare these quantities to some, existing standard. The first step in this aspect of measurement was already taken as we organized data in preparation for this act. Our next logical course of action would be to determine what standards should serve as our primary means of evaluation. Again, part of this has been completed if the recommendation to establish benchmarks to coincide with our KPI selections was fulfilled.

Although we have, in essence, already performed the measurement step within the web analytics process, we will expand upon some of the intermittent steps that have already taken place. Further, we will discuss some new measurement related topics and provide more detail on others that were alluded to earlier. The proceeding subjects will serve to fill any remaining gaps as we march toward the end of the web analytics process.

Calculating Conversion Rates

Many of the activities serving as the focal point of our web analytics' measurement efforts may have already been quantified within our new set of organized data. A major element within this part of the process is to calculate any conversion rate metrics chosen to serve as key performance indicators within our own process. Conversions themselves are represented by straight counts similar to the metrics utilized in performance measurement. Conversion rates involve a degree of data manipulation to determine a percentage rate of activity for use in comparison to standards. Their important roles within the web analytics process has already been clearly stated but let us take an expanded view to ensure that your own conversion metrics reflect the results needed.

On many occasions, we have stressed the importance of utilizing metrics that are clearly defined and easy to understand. Calculated conversion rates, by their very nature will fall into this category. As previously noted, they are a measurement of a specific activity or action as a percentage of page or site traffic in their most basic form. Conversion rates are calculated simply by dividing the number of specific actions that occurred over a defined period (typically one month) using the total pageviews, visits or unique visitors on a given page or across the entire site during that same period. As you can see, we are dealing with simple arithmetic here but the result is an expression of outcomes relative to web site traffic with direct ties to why the site exists in the first place.

Justifying the Use of Traffic Data

So why measure these outcomes as a percentage of traffic? The one universal action that any user performs on your web property is simply visiting it. Whether they look at one page or several, whether they start on the homepage or begin on a specific sub page, it is the one action that drives all of the other activities that may occur within the site. This quality also makes web site and page traffic the easiest means with which to impact our conversions when a need to influence them is required. Want to sell more products? The first thing to look at is to increase site traffic. Of course, this is an extremely simplistic view but it does stand up in support of the logic behind calculating conversions in this style.

So which traffic measure should I use? It is easy to rationalize the utilization of each; pageviews, unique visitors and visits. Also, you can reasonably argue looking at new visits, total time spent or employ total traffic from a distinct, audience segment. However, your own answer will again lie within the objectives and goals originally identified as pertaining to your site and the very nature of the activity being measured itself.

Start by looking at the specific activity that you are seeking to measure. If it is the purchase of a product, does your site offer just one item that consists of only a single, final transaction? If so, then look at which traffic metric is the most relevant to this action being performed. Does a user having a single or several pageviews impact the likelihood of the transaction? How about whether they visit more than once? In truth, both of these potential calculations can provide needed insight but in this case, we would probably start with unique visitors. How many of the total number of people visiting our site during the defined reporting period actually bought a product. This is the most easily understood metric we can use in this particular case. If you are unsure which traffic measure to employ, follow the logic laid out above to make your decision.

Unique Visitors will win out in such arguments more often than not when just getting started with analytics. Begin with this when first formulating your conversion rates as it is the most direct correlation when measuring actual user actions that can be performed on a site (i.e. buying products, completing forms, submitting emails etc.).

When calculating conversion rates for more indirect actions such as visiting a particular content page, employing total pageviews as the sub divider is a good place to start. Whether the engagement tally is derived from the number of visits, unique visitors to a page or is comprised of one of the social media metrics defined earlier, the argument made in favor of traffic metric use holds true. Pageviews are recommended here for their ability to more directly reflect engagement versus a count of the number of unique visitors. The reason for this lies in the way a pageview is actually counted. One is recorded only after the entire web page has been downloaded to the user screen. While this may only take a few seconds in many cases, it does stand to confirm that an opportunity to engage with the content did occur. In contrast, a unique visitor may be counted as arriving at the page but may have immediately moved on before any "engagement" took place.

Understand that the use of traffic metrics as the denominator in any conversion rate calculation is not absolute. Furthermore, the suggestions made above are meant to facilitate adoption and proper calculation rather than represent any hard line rules. While the vast majority of conversions can be calculated using the methodology just discussed there some specific cases that demonstrate alternative forms of conversion metrics. We will address some of these next.

Beyond Standard Conversion Rates

In the next chapter we will look more deeply into the actual analysis of our collected and calculated measurement data. There, more meaningful insight will be derived from our chosen conversion rates and may uncover a need to adjust existing key performance indicators or expand their use to better answer questions derived from the presented results. We can address some of this now by presenting some additional metric possibilities that are intended to serve a more supplemental role to the standard conversion rates. Likewise, detailing them and their use here can serve to mitigate some future need for metric adjustment or expansion or may add to our current list of key performance indicators.

Time Or Visits To Purchase: Earlier, we cited a metric's ability to span multiple reporting periods as an additional factor in selecting or designing key performance metrics. Standard conversion rates express outcomes as a percentage of traffic pertaining only to a single period. On occasion, information that spans multiple periods is required to supplement or explain standard conversion results in the current period. Counting the number of visits a particular user makes before committing to a purchase (or any other direct act) serves in this capacity through various forms.

Assigning and tracking visits to individual users is a function that may not be available in some of the more common tracking tools. Options with more advanced capabilities like Omniture will definitely allow this tracking but we can implement another alternative for cases in which this level of detail is not possible. A web site average pertaining to the number of visits required in lieu of a purchase or other action can be calculated as follows:

Visits / # of purchases

Visits / # of downloads

While this may lack the accuracy reflected in the direct assignment and counting of visits by purchasing users it can still provide some similar insight while forgoing a larger commitment to tracking resources. It also serves as an example of a conversion metric that does not employ a common traffic metric as a denominator. Here, we are using the conversion count itself.

User Loyalty: Retention rate was defined as a measure of the number of repeat visits occurring as a percentage against total visits to the web site. We classified this metric as one put into common use but failed to identify it as an actual conversion rate. In truth, if repeat visitation is one of the key actions that a web site was created to foster, the retention rate metric can be viewed as more of a conversion type metric. Each instance where a user has opted to return to the web site after their initial visit represents a conversion to some degree.

This can be taken a step further by viewing information within your tacking tool that segments repeat visits by their frequency providing much greater insight into the loyalty exhibited by the site's user base. Such information can be utilized as a supplement to more standard conversion rates or stand on their own as a segmented version of retention conversions.

Bounce Rate: This was characterized earlier as representing the failure rate of a given web site. Though its calculation is often performed for you through the common tracking tools, the resulting percentage represents the ratio of single pageview visits versus total site visits. This determination is arrived at using a similar methodology to the one suggested for the more standard conversion types. However, bounce rate, as a measure of failure does not represent a rate of conversion. Instead, we mention it here as its inverse could be interpreted as yet another outcome measure for use in supplementing our other metrics.

If, for example, a web site currently has a bounce rate of 20%, this means that two out of every ten visits result in a user's immediate departure. What we can also derive from this metric is the fact that eight of every ten visits resulted in a greater degree of engagement as evidenced by the user's generation of multiple pageviews during their visit. This can be argued as a measure of conversion albeit a very broad one. It serves to supplement the more standard conversion rates as one correlates changes in it to potential changes in other, more direct conversion measures.

Task Completion Rate: When a web site is offering multiple forms of conversion, it may prove useful to compare the occurrence of each individual "task" against the sum total of all potential options. This sum total represents the combined counts of all targeted or desired actions and produces a percentage of occurrences for each specific conversion as follows:

# of downloads / Sum total of all conversions

This calculation does offer another example of a potential conversion rate that does not employ traffic metrics as a denominator. It also finds value only as a supplement to more standard conversion rates as it will quickly identify those conversions that the web site is generating the most.

Later Adjustment Needs

We can start with calculating the conversion rates that make the most sense relative to our reporting needs now. There is no need to go beyond the standard conversion rate types if doing so only serves to complicate your own process. When we revisit them during our discussion on deeper analysis, your chosen metrics will either be confirmed as is or identified as needing some adjustment to garner the insights we need. Remember, web analytics is best viewed as a fluid activity, especially when first getting started. The act of reviewing and manipulating data can lead to new points of view that result in changes to what is most important relative measuring performance. With this in mind, we can move on to our next measurement subject.

Economic Value

Throughout our discussion of web analytics, we have yet to call attention to the assignment of an economic value to the various metrics being employed in our measurement efforts. This last subject pertaining to the ascertainment of the quantities related to our key performance indicators involves assigning a dollar (or other currency) value to our chosen metrics.

Facilitate Use in External Reporting

 Converting metrics into a form that reflects economic value does not necessarily represent an imperative that is critical to the success of our web analytics process. Web sites that do not directly sell products or offer purchasable ad space may not have need for such a conversion. However, when we reflect on the use of key performance indicators within external reporting, we must recognize that an expression of those results in more economic terms may be needed after all.

Consider web sites designed to support a sales team by providing more detailed information to potential customers. Nothing may be sold directly through the site but it certainly does play a role in generating sales for the organization, at least indirectly. In this example, the KPIs employed are likely focused on measuring engagement type activities and do not lend themselves to easy assignment of economic value. However, it is possible to tie engagement results to outside sales by connecting shifts in engagement to shifts in the organization's sales. When engagement increases online, a corresponding increase in sales should be evident. This connection may not always materialize in such an obvious way but increasing the span of web data to include multiple periods should diminish this.

Return on Investment

Return on investment describes the rate of return one has received from an initial outlay of financial resources. This can be construed as yet another performance measure of a web site, especially if its creation required some monetary investment. Furthermore, a web site's operation and maintenance requires the allocation of resources within an organization and like an initial investment, justify a need to measure their related costs against the value generated by the web site.

Again, e-commerce and advertising web site's lend themselves well to the determination of return on investment as they generate revenue directly. The dollars derived from product and ad sales can be quickly compared to any investment or resource allocation expense to measure return. Other types of web sites will require some more work to assign an economic value to their targeted outcomes but an avenue is available as evidenced by the example in the last section. For additional clarification, consider a web site intended to garner client registrations. These are collected through the completion of an online form and represent one of the primary means of conversion on the site. Client information from the completed forms is collected in another department's database and is used to facilitate initial contact as part of a longer sales cycle performed outside of the online operation.

Assigning economic value to the form completion conversions requires a sales number attributed directly to this online effort. However, not all conversions result in sales and they certainly do not correspond to the same period in which the original form completion took place. What is called for here is direct assistance from this other department for a means to tie these online conversions to a sales value. It is likely that they do perform their own performance measurements that, with a little tweaking, can be applied to the situation detailed here.

Reaching out to the other department produces an average sale conversion rate of 20% related to leads generated online. Although this revenue is not collected in the same period as the online conversion itself, this matter is tabled for the sake of simplicity in assigning an economic value to web site operations. In addition to a 20% close rate, an organization wide, average sales value of $100 is provided. We assign an economic value to the form completion conversions as follows:

# of conversions x 0.20 x 100

Our result is an estimated value of the conversions counted in any given period. In turn, this new dollar value assigned to one of the primary target operations of the web site can be utilized to determine the return on any investment or resource allocation cost incurred.

Measurement Supplement

The examples presented within the external reporting and return on investment sections are interchangeable and can represent the assignment of economic value for any purpose. In each case, they resulted in a conversion value and this can serve as a supplemental metric for use in the later analysis phase of the web analytics process.

Average Conversion Value: Regardless of the action or activity being measured, its adaptation to reflect a monetary form of measurement can be employed to supplement our more standard conversion calculations. Consider a situation where a particular, standard rate is deemed to be relatively low. Normally, this would signal a need to take action to reverse fortunes and improve on this result. However, in this same situation, the calculated conversion value is much higher than average. Fewer conversions occurred but the impact on revenue remained unchanged or even improved. Conversely, a high standard conversion rate could correspond to a lower average conversion value and equally result in a misinterpretation of what is actually happening on the web site.

By looking at conversion through a different lens, a very different picture can emerge relative to the actual performance of the web site. Assigning an economic value involves the quantification of our metrics through a different means but this effort can lead us to a similar end.

Role of Historical Data

We have successfully expanded upon the measurement component pertaining to the ascertainment of quantity and will now turn our attention to the equally important comparison with an existing standard to complete our discussion. Previously, we mentioned assigning benchmarks to our selected key performance indicators. These were cited as an important contributor to the make-up of an effective KPI metric and represent our first development of a standard value with which to compare performance results.

Refer back to the two subdivisions of data cited in the last chapter; current and historical. The process of measurement within the web analytics process involves the comparison of current period data with historical results from earlier periods. In this fashion, historical data serves as the primary source of those standards needed to complete the measurement process. It is in this capacity that historical data performs its role and is the first and best option to establish baselines of performance to measure current results.

The effectiveness of this effort will be determined by how far back our existing historical data can reach. Ideally, we will have 2-3 years of data with which to work from in order to derive our performance standards. However, it is entirely possible that one may not have the luxury of access to extensive historical data. The web site may have just launched or this data may not have been collected and saved in the past. If this is the case, the focus will shift to building credible historical information with which to compare our web property's future performance.

Establishing and Comparing to Our Base Performance Levels

The establishment of historical performance standards or baselines represents the most fundamental aspect of our web analytics process to date. We alter past data first by organizing it in a consistent manner to match with current results. We then manipulate past data into standard averages or ranges that mirror those measurements that we deemed most relevant to our current performance.

For each current key performance indicator, a standard of performance is set in the form of an average or range of values. The span of activity reflected in the newly created standard should match the reporting time period expressed in our current data. If one month increments are used to define reporting periods, the baseline comparison value should provide a monthly historical average or range of performance. This baseline will serve as the first comparison opportunity when measuring current data results.

If the existing depth of historical information allows, annual performance averages can be calculated to supplement the monthly standard. Furthermore, it is important to note that the calculation of monthly or annual performance averages and ranges does not spell the end of the historical data's use. The details that comprise these averages across each prior reporting period will play a significant role as measurement moves from this first step to more in depth comparison and subsequent analysis.

Creating Value

Key performance indicators offer little value in and of themselves unless a corresponding standard with which to compare is assigned to them. Their establishment and use will foster such questions as:

Did our overall traffic continue to rise or fall?

Has there been any change in the number of conversions the site is garnering?

Did the activity level on that particular content page change?

Without the means to compare results to a reliable standard, the ability to derive insight and greater understanding does not exist. Getting three thousand unique visitors this month does not mean much unless viewed from the context of what the web site did before.

Circumstances may preclude you from utilizing historical data to calculate historical performance standards. This apparent problem does not have to stop your own web analytics efforts in its tracks. Next, we will discuss an alternative source for standard performance baselines in the form of competitive intelligence.

Competitive Intelligence

In the absence of any extensive historical data, competitive intelligence can be collected to formulate those critical performance standards needed to complete the measurement process. Some information on your web site's competition may already exist. Often, this type of market research is employed before and during the development of a site and should be reviewed to see if any information can be applied to formulate performance standards.

Admittedly, data that reflects actual competitor web site performance will be difficult to come by. They will certainly not offer up this kind of information with any degree of detail. However, some tools are available to augment any existing competitive knowledge or be used to create the initial performance standards needed in our own measurement efforts.

Google Trends for Websites

Google Trends for Websites is a very useful in finding out the traffic data and geographic visitation patterns of competitor web sites. By entering the URL address, a graph will be shown that reflects the number of daily unique visitors of that given web site.

Attention Meter

This tool allows you to enter up to five domains and offers a quick snapshot of traffic data, with graphs supplied from Alexa, Compete, and QuantCast.

Statbrain

Fill in a form on the Statbrain page and you instantly find out how many visits any competing web site has. This works by tapping different resources across the Web and combining them using algorithms to produce an estimate of the number of visits a website receives.

Compete

Compete is another option that allows for the entering of a URL to learn basic traffic and rankings of competitive web sites. Its "pro" offering can be subscribed to access a much richer set of data.

Quantcast

This free tool provides one of today's most accurate audience measurement services. With the Marketer Checklist, you get to build detailed audience profiles and define the most receptive customer segments. You can also find similar audiences across the Web that "look like" those already interacting with or targeted by your site.

Quarkbase

This quick and comprehensive tool gives information on a web site's traffic data, related sites, social comments, description and social popularity. You can also search top web sites by different categories.

When All Else Fails

The above list of competitive intelligence tools is by no means comprehensive but does represent an adequate set of resources when seeking to establish performance standards to measure web site performance. However, many of the key performance indicators that were selected for your own process may be tracking activity that such tools simply do not cover. When all else fails, the best option for establishing baseline performance standards rests in the creation of minimal operational guidelines.

What do we mean by this? Decide on a minimum level of performance in which the web site can operate and still be viewed as acceptable. Of course, this will prove to be very subjective but any determinations can serve as baseline standards in the absence of any derived from historical results or competitive and market information. When specifically looking at conversions, remember the fact that most typically perform at a rate of one to three percent. Start there while more accurate and reliable data is collected during the first weeks and months of your web site's operation.

Did you convert any chosen metrics to reflect their estimated, economic value? Use these amounts and calculate what levels of conversion activity are needed to break even relative to any investment or resource allocation expense. Although the employment of any of these most recent suggestions may result in a degree of questionable accuracy relative to current performance, their intent is to only fill the gap and allow for some meaningful comparison until enough historical data has been collected.

Summary Outline

Measurement

- Measurement is a process defined by the ascertainment of quantities and their comparison to an existing standard
- Much of the measurement portion of the web analytics process has likely already been completed

Calculating Conversion Rates

- Conversions and conversion rate metrics will account for the majority of KPIs utilized within the web analytics process
- Their calculation often consists of simple arithmetic
- The key aspect in their calculation rests with the denominator chosen
- Traffic metrics represent the most common sub dividers in use within web analytics
- Some additional, non-standard conversion rates may prove useful during data analysis
- Future efforts can uncover a need to adjust selection and calculation of current conversion rates

Economic Value

- Although not always critical, assigning an economic value to KPIs can be justified

- Expressing metrics in economic terms helps to ease their inclusion in various, external reports published within the wider organization
- A need to calculate a return on investment will call for a monetary value transition
- Assigned monetary values can serve to supplement more standard conversion metrics by offering an alternative view of performance

Role of Historical Data

- Historical data is utilized to establish standard baselines of performance with which to compare current results
- Effectiveness is determined by the depth of historical information available
- These established standards are reflected as averages and should correspond with current data organization to facilitate comparison
- The value of KPIs is derived directly from the existence of a standard with which to compare too

Competitive Intelligence

- Competitor data offers an alternative to historical data when the later is not available
- Several resources are available to augment current competitive data or to create initial standards for use in the measurement process

When All Else Fails

- Conversion standards are difficult to replicate in the absence of historical data
- Many of the competitive intelligence tools do not offer this kind of detail
- The only other option is to decide upon a minimum acceptable level of performance
- Any of these standard establishment alternatives are intended only to fill the gap until enough historical data has been collected

Recommended Exercises:

1. Calculate conversion rates.

2. Calculate any needed standard performance baselines for each KPI.

Chapter 8

Quantitative Data Analysis

Leveraging quantitative data to uncover the "why"

Why We Test

What to Look for

Predictive Analytics

Factors to Consider in Predictive Analytics

When Quantitative Analysis Is Not Enough

Leveraging Quantitative Information

In the last chapter, we discussed the fundamental components of measurement and the value and importance of comparing our current data with some existing standard to judge web site performance. Measuring key performance indicators in this manner forms the basis for much of the remaining aspects of our web analytics efforts. Comparing collected metric quantities to established standard performance levels allows one to derive the insights needed to better understand a web site's performance and make more informed business decisions.

The next series of topics will articulate the procedures and techniques needed to perform a deeper analysis of the quantitative data that the preceding steps have identified, collected and measured. Our focus will begin with the recognition of movement or fluctuation within the current results of our key performance indicators. We will then leverage the data in order to seek explanations as to why these changes may have occurred.

Material Levels of Change

Whether we are looking at a long history of web traffic results or reviewing data from the site's first few weeks, the first step in our quantitative analysis centers on identifying material levels of change. We define this as changes in current results versus those from the past that are significant enough to warrant attention. What qualifies as significant can be considered largely subjective depending on the nature of your site, the time period in question, the metrics involved and your own level of comfort in the fluctuation of data points from period to period.

As a rule of thumb, it is recommended that a 10% or greater change in any metric be investigated more closely. This number is somewhat arbitrary but represents an immediate starting point when first beginning. It is also very easy to determine and does not require a separate calculation when performing your initial review. Drop one decimal position from any given number and you have your 10% amount (i.e. 5052 to 505). After quickly perusing your data, you may note that a lower material rate is needed. If so, make a judgment call on your own. The established performance standards assigned to each KPI serve as the means of comparison in this exercise to determine what amount of change in your metrics is deemed significant.

Before moving forward, be sure to consider a few more factors to weigh what might be a material change in performance for your web site. First, consider the span of your historical data utilized in standard establishment for the purpose of data comparison. In statistics, larger fluctuations in data tend to even out over time. If you are working with historical data going back only a month or less, it is likely that you will see a good deal of volatility relative to your results. As the span of historical data lengthens, large fluctuations should theoretically decrease. We should not ignore such large swings in the short term but keep this in perspective and view them in the context described above. In cases where alternative standard development was employed, base any decisions relative to material change on the level of comfort you have in their accuracy or reliability.

 Second, be sure to consider the nature of your web site and its array of activities and functions offered to potential users. The hope is that the existing historical data will have provided a clear understanding as to how your particular web site can be expected to work. Larger fluctuations may be common or at least easy to explain based on more typical user behavior reflected within the past results. Again, the depth of past information available will play a role but it can alter the definition of what is material in either direction.

Lastly, take a user-centric approach when assessing how to define a significant amount of change. In other words, try and put yourself in the shoes of a visitor to your site. Do the actions or activities that you would perform as a site user help explain why certain fluctuations occur? While this method is less than scientific, it can help in gaining new perspective on your performance results and has been and will be referred to again later in the web analytics process.

Determining what level of change should be deemed material and significant is a subjective exercise. Different organizations, different types of sites and different reporting needs all coalesce to create this circumstance. However, regardless of the situation, what metric fluctuations are considered significant and worthy of deeper investigation will be become clearer through continual application and experience.

Report Tip

To help facilitate this analysis, it is recommended that a new column or row, depending on the format of your central reporting document be added. A rate calculation subtracting the past average result from the current actual result and then further subdividing that amount by the past average result $(X-Y) / X$ will provide a percentage change for that metric. This simple automation technique will reduce this effort and foster a quick review making multiple month or even yearly comparisons easy.

The Detail Behind Standard Baselines

Comparison of the quantitative data from the current reporting period to those established performance averages or ranges represent an opening step. When these comparisons yield a material difference, a signal is given to analyze the results in greater detail. As was alluded to in the last chapter, the detail behind the standard performance averages can be tapped to expand upon this initial comparison and allow for a deeper investigation.

Recall the recommendation to create standards of comparison in a form that mirrors the reporting period of the current KPI data being measured. The purpose of this was to better facilitate a quick and accurate comparison to judge performance. While this exercise may signal a need for further investigation, the very nature of these standards may preclude the development of any further insight into the reasons why a material difference may exist. For this reason, the usefulness of our collected historical data, in all of its detail, is made clear.

If the span of our historical data allows, we do not stop at just a single period of comparison but instead access the finer details related to the metric in question. We start by looking further back into the historic results that were already organized in a consistent fashion with our current data to see if this variation is part of a longer term trend or represents a one time occurrence. Using the report tip from the last section, the original average can be compared to all prior reporting period results to amplify the potential insight that can be derived.

Trends

As was just explained, our more detailed historical data can be tapped in an effort to uncover any existing trends that may be employed to explain the current results.

Initially, it is recommended to allocate more energy to negative movement versus positive but understanding reasons for both is important in our continued effort to measure web site performance.

There is no standard definition of what qualifies as a trend in web analytics but any demonstrated consistency occurring over three or more periods should suffice. If a trend has materialized, we need to look at a few key aspects to garner further insight. Whether positive or negative, what is the trend showing us? Are the percentage changes consistent throughout the trend? If so, your focus should turn to the likely occurrence of an event, site change or series of both that caused this consistent drop or rise in your measured activities. A consistent rise is what we are always hoping for and finding a good explanation as to why this is happening can provide insight into the establishment of a new best practice. A consistent fall is of more concern and is indicative of the recurrence of an issue or effect that is negatively impacting our site's performance. Regardless, the best action is to review the period in which the trend started to see if a cause can be identified.

What if the percentage changes are not regular over the course of the existing trend?

Often the numbers do not lend themselves to such uniform patterns and we may be faced with a rather inconsistent trend. In general, web activity is very dynamic and this is reflected in potentially volatile swings in the recorded metric measurements of any given property. A trend may not be readily apparent at first glance because of this fact but a previous tip can be applied here. Looking at our historical data over a greater span of time is appropriate when more straightforward trends are not evident. Remember, we mentioned that fluctuations in data tend to even out more over the course of time. Remain cognizant of this fact when searching for a possible trend to explain a current rise or fall in performance. To clarify, did a particular KPI demonstrate a negative result compared to the baseline average eight out of the last twelve months? Furthermore, did the majority of positive or negative trend components occur earlier or later in the year? We cannot always expect our results to fit neatly into easily recognizable trends but we can certainly garner some indication of where our performance is heading by looking at a wider range of data.

Another useful comparison, when the data is available, is to look at that particular period's performance compared to the same time in the prior year. Instead of a month to month trend, maybe one exists that is expressed as an annual occurrence. Perform this exercise over as many years as the data allows in order to see what insights it might produce. Again, the report tip mentioned at the end of the material change section can prove useful here and another can be added to assist in the spotting of trends.

Report Tip 2

When faced with inconsistency relative to trends, one can more easily spot them across a longer period by converting KPI metric data into a charted format. Within Excel, a chart can be created using the current and past results data to create a trend line that represents each monthly result over an extended period of time. This resulting visual aid will provide a clearer indication of whether a trend does in fact exist when a review of the quantitative data bears no fruit.

Regardless of the type or nature of the trend, we direct our focus on them for one, primary reason. They allow us to quickly pinpoint where the potential cause of our current state may have occurred. While we seek to understand why a particular material change has happened we are, in essence, trying to establish some kind of cause and effect relationship. That cause may be a specific event, a change implemented within our site or the materialization of a new user behavior being reflected in our results. Narrowing our search for these at the beginning of a trend should help in their discovery and may even make identification quite obvious. When the cause is not readily apparent, narrowing down to a relevant time in which it may have occurred will still prove useful.

Cause and Effect

We discussed the study of trends as our first step in seeking understanding as to why a key performance metric has fallen or risen compared to historic results. This allows us to narrow down the list of potential causes if we cannot recognize them outright. We loosely define the when so we can move on to figuring out the why by asking: Why did this effect occur? What event or action was the cause?

Quantitative data from other key performance indicators or from metrics outside of them can be used to identify causes. For example, a drop in the number of form completion conversions might be easily explained by a corresponding drop in web site traffic. In turn, this drop in web site traffic might be explained by a decrease in the number of referrals received from search engines or other web sites. Noting this, it is determined that the most recent search campaign implemented on behalf of the site had ended, impacting the level of traffic referrals received by one of the major search engines. As you can see, the application of cause and effect analysis serves to narrow the list of reasons down until a root basis can be easily identified.

This supports the use of the cause and effect approach for its simplicity and ease of understanding. This holds true even when multiple causes could be at play like the brief example detailed above. We continually apply the cause and effect analysis like peeling the layers off of an onion until our need for the understanding of the performance result is satisfied.

General Tips to Aid Quantitative Analysis

Despite the simplicity evident in the cause and effect approach, the actual type of potential causes that may be derived will again prove to be subjective. This fact makes it impossible to provide a complete list of causes that your quantitative analysis might uncover. However, some general tips can be provided to augment your ability to identify these types of relationships.

Adjust your material level of change standard over time. When just starting out in web analytics, the percentage of change selected is rather arbitrary. Over time, your results will reflect more consistent patterns and your target level for investigation should be adjusted accordingly.

Consider the depth of your historical information when comparing to current results. Not all will have the luxury of years of organized data with which to compare to current performance. This fact and its impact have been referenced on numerous occasions already. When the depth is limited or non-existent, temper any conclusions reached when conducting your initial analysis. Three months is a bare minimum and the most reliable insights are drawn from data going back much further by several months or years.

Newly launched sites offer a unique set of causes with which to start. Often, a brand new web site will not have the luxury of lengthy spans of historical data. Despite this, analysis of results is extremely important as was alluded to in earlier chapters. Do not panic at the site of negative results but take care to investigate larger movement early. Cause and effect relationship analysis is aided given the fact that they are likely to have spawned directly from issues arising during the web site's development. They may be technical in nature or reflect a miscalculation relative to the user experience of the web property. Catching such issues is the primary focus of analysis when just getting launched and should dominate the list of resulting causes.

Metrics showing zero results for the current period. When a specific traffic metric has fallen to zero during a given reporting period consider investigating the existence of a tracking problem first. A zero pageview count will often prove to be an indicator as it should lead to zero visits and unique visitors as well.

If your site is not new but has undergone a significant redesign, treat it as a new site from a web analytics perspective. The historical data from the previous site version is still relevant but must be viewed in a different light when major changes are implemented. Subsequent results and trends are very likely caused by the change in the user environment and are affecting the behavior of your visitor base. You are no longer comparing "apples to apples" so to speak. Instead focus your cause analysis around the changes that were implemented and on how they may have impacted user behavior in the new environment.

Identify best practices. In a perfect world, all of our measurements demonstrate a positive trend. If you are so lucky to find yourself in this circumstance, seek a better understanding as to why this is happening. In other words, utilize cause and effect relationship analysis to try and identify any best practices in your web site's layout or offerings that can be applied elsewhere or focused upon to maintain momentum.

Identify engagement related causes through article tracking results. It is possible to track individual blog and news articles that you may be publishing on your site or elsewhere. This is set up within the various web traffic tracking tools in the same fashion as your regular site pages. Doing so allows for the comparison of different articles with an eye toward identifying reasons for changes in engagement through individual and collective article traffic performance.

Utilize traffic source data to determine potential causes. Similar to the example detailed in the cause and effect section, a review of the various sources of your web site traffic can provide needed insight during an investigation. Better yet, establish some baseline rates of contribution from the various search engines and web sites that consistently appear within your traffic data.

Look for special relationships between the various key performance indicators that you are tracking. Sometimes, seemingly unrelated actions or activities in one area have a large impact on another. For example, a drop in one conversion metric may always correspond to a drop or rise in another. Test any hypothesis through more thorough analysis of your historical data and note for future reference any newly discovered correlations.

Reference the bounce rate report to explain any fluctuations on an individual page or across the entire site. We have already defined this metric and called out its potential use as a supplemental report. It is here where its usefulness can be experienced as a potential cause explaining movement relative to your key performance indicators. A high percentage for the site or a particular page indicates that it is not meeting user expectations upon their initial visit. Remember too that its inverse can be used to explain more positive results.

Analyze site conversions using both a straight count and calculated rate against overall traffic. When used in tandem, these two methods of conversion tracking can simplify the cause and effect relationship investigation. A consistent change in the results of both methods indicates a cause that does not relate directly to current traffic levels. Conversely, a change in one method's results but not the other can usually be attributed to web site traffic.

Whenever you are aware of the timing of a change implementation, note the date and search your results data for any metric movement. In addition, be sure to note the logic behind the implementation as this will improve your analysis of the metric results that follow. In these cases, your cause is already known and your efforts are centered on understanding the actual impact. However, it is important that you look beyond any areas known to be directly affected as unexpected influence relative to other metrics is possible.

Testing

The last tip we discussed offers an excellent segue into another key area of quantitative web traffic analysis; testing. Before any major changes to a site are implemented, organizations will often first test different variations of the proposed alteration in order to measure its effect on the site's performance. Different options are activated only to a small portion of the total audience and related metrics are analyzed over a period of time to assess the impact of each variation. Such tests are run until a reasonable understanding of how performance will be impacted is reached.   The best option is then chosen for full implementation across the web site.

As you can see, we start with a cause (proposed change) first and look to determine what effects it has by analyzing our performance results. This represents an inverse to the more standard cause and effect relationship analysis described earlier. Although we start from the opposite end, insight is garnered in the same fashion as more standard results analysis. One key difference here is that we are only allowing a small percentage of our regular audience (no more than 5-10%) to respond to the various changes and avoid disrupting our site's primary performance. So this analysis only applies to a sub set of the larger, current data pool.

Types of web site testing that you may have heard about already include the following:

A/B Testing

In its most rudimentary form, A/B testing involves determining the better of two different content variables. More often, this type of testing can be characterized by a structure in which a baseline control sample is compared to a variety of single-variable test samples in order to measure affects.

Multivariate Testing

Multivariate testing is a process by which more than one component of a website may be tested in a live environment. It can be thought of in simple terms as numerous A/B tests performed on one page at the same time. Limitations on the number of combinations and variables in such a test are determined by the amount of time it will take to get enough data to reach a valid conclusion and computational resources. Multivariate testing encompasses a far more advanced testing method and its use by one beginning in web analytics is likely minimal.

Why We Test

Significant results can be seen through the testing of various elements like copy text, links, page layouts, navigation changes, image use and colors. Not all elements produce the same degree of impact and by looking at the results from different tests; it is possible to identify those elements that consistently tend to produce the highest level of change in our metric results.

What To Watch Out For

When performing a controlled test you are seeking to document the effects or changes within your key performance indicators or other metrics after the implementation of the new variables. Whether comparing results between two options or several variations against the current version (control), the focus is on identifying shifts in those performance results and selecting the variation that demonstrates the most improvement.

There are no standards of time with which to run tests based on the variables you are testing but their length should be based on the length needed to collect enough data to make a comfortable decision. Again, we have another subjective decision in front of us but successful tests usually do not require a great amount of time. If you do not have the ability to perform a test to only a portion of the existing audience, consider shortening the length of the test if the results are showing an adverse effect on overall site performance.

One final factor to consider when performing a test is to pay attention to all existing KPIs regardless of their direct ties to any of the variables involved. It is common to encounter unexpected shifts in areas that seemingly have no direct connection to those variables being altered in the test. While the metrics that were expected to improve may have done so, this may have occurred at the expense of another in an unforeseen manner.

Predictive Analytics

Testing can be viewed as a means to provide insight into what our future results will be if any of the variables in consideration are chosen. Often, we may have a need to employ our metric data to provide a window into the future and predict what can be expected of our performance results. Performing such an exercise in web analytics is not unlike the efforts undertaken by a sales department to forecast revenue or a finance team to project income. However, predictive analytics can involve a high degree of sophistication and employ a great deal of resources that many individuals and organizations cannot access. While more intense predictive efforts can result in more accuracy or reliability within their forecasts, even a beginner can utilize quantitative analytics data to produce some predictive results.

Performing quantitative analysis through identification of cause and effect relationships will result in greater understanding of why specific results occur. This will serve to improve the level of comfort one will have in what performance outcomes to expect, especially as more reporting periods come and go. Furthermore, as we review historic data and its details looking for trends we can use this information not only to locate causes but to forecast where our site performance might be headed.

As an example, consider a web site that has been demonstrating a fairly consistent level of performance for several months. It would be reasonable to assume that this trend will continue barring any unexpected user behavior or general market shifts. A continuation of this consistent performance can be forecasted. However, what if some changes were planned to jumpstart a new growth trend? If testing is performed prior to the final decision, those indicators demonstrated during the test can be applied to predict an increase in overall performance after the new change or changes are implemented.

Certain web site types like those dedicated to e-commerce or the sale of advertising space will rely on predictive analytics to a greater degree. When product sales are a focal point, existing forecasting methods from the organization's sales department can likely be applied to predict online sales results. In their absence, the more basic method described above can be applied to meet what will surely be a common analytics need for this kind of site. Those that sell ad space will do so using forecasts of future impressions (and sometimes clicks or other measures) that serve as inventory estimates for future advertisers. Media campaigns that include digital advertising are rarely purchased in real time so a need for predictive analytics results is paramount.

Factors to Consider in Predictive Analytics

Regardless of the reason driving the need to predict future results of the web site, a few simple factors can be reviewed to better facilitate the predictive process and assess the reliability or accuracy of the results.

Depth of existing historic data

Current degree of understanding and control of performance results

How far in the future predicted results will span

Degree to which factors outside one's control may occur

Existence of planned changes

Span of current, discovered trends

Volatility of typical performance results

This list may not encompass all of the factors to be considered when employing quantitative results to predict or forecast future results but it should be enough to reasonably gauge reliability and enhance the ability to decide whether to move forward or not.

When Quantitative Analysis Is Not Enough

We have demonstrated a simple methodology to analyze your quantitative data as a means to understand the nature behind our current and future performance results. However, investigating quantitative data has its limits and you may encounter a need to look beyond the numbers to explain why a particular outcome has occurred. To complete the analysis process, the application of qualitative data will be essential to ensure that a true understanding of what our data results are saying is achieved.

In the next chapter, we will look at various qualitative factors that can be included within our web analytics process to enhance our ability to identify causes and explain their effects relative to web site performance.

Summary Outline

Leveraging Quantitative Information

- A deeper analysis of our quantitative data is performed to seek answers as to why certain results occurred

Material Levels of Change

- Attention is focused on those KPIs showing a high degree of change when compared to baseline standards
- Deciding on what is material is subjective but a 10% degree of change can serve as a good starting point
- Any metrics demonstrating a material level of change are targeted for further investigation as to why

The Detail Behind Standard Baselines

- Review of the historic details that comprise our baseline standards serve as the first stop in a deeper investigation into material changes
- When available, this detail allows for multiple period comparisons as answers are sought

Trends

- Reviewing historic data allows for the identification of performance trends that can be used to explain current results
- As a general rule, similar results occurring over a period of two to three months or greater qualify as a trend but can be broken down to weeks and days if shorter time frames are being analyzed
- Discovering the beginning of a trend will narrow focus on what event or change occurred to start the trend in the first place
- Trends are not always obvious but increasing the span of time we are analyzing or employing other techniques can facilitate their discovery

Cause and Effect

- As we seek greater understanding as to why our results have risen or fallen, we are in essence seeking a direct cause and effect relationship.
- It works well in web analytics for its simplicity and ease of understanding both during our investigation and later as we communicate findings.
- Causes common to your own site will again prove to be rather subjective.

General Tips to Aid Quantitative Analysis

- Adjust your material level of change over time
- Consider the depth of your historical data when conducting comparisons to current results
- Newly launched sites lack historical data making the need for current results analysis all the more important
- Metrics suddenly dropping to zero in a given reporting period may indicate a reporting/technical issue
- Treat redesigned sites as entirely new when comparing to the previous version's historical data

- Identify best practices when faced with consistent, positive comparison results
- Identify engagement related causes through article tracking results
- Utilize traffic source data to determine potential causes
- Look for special relationships between the various key performance indicators that you are tracking
- Reference the bounce rate report to explain any fluctuations on an individual page or across the entire site
- Analyze site conversions using both a straight count and calculated rate against overall traffic
- When a change implementation is planned, be prepared to measure results with that specific cause in mind.

Testing

- Testing represents an inverse to the standard cause and effect analysis, the cause is known so measuring the effects becomes the focus
- Test types include A/B and multivariate
- We perform tests to identify the variables that produce the best results
- We look for shifts in current metric results caused by the changes being tested
- Need to include monitoring of all KPIs as change can occur even when no direct tie to the test variable is evident
- The length of a test is subjective but should be concluded once enough information to make a decision has been achieved

Predictive Analytics

- Quantitative data can be used to forecast future results
- Because of their nature, e-commerce and advertising web sites require the use of predictive analytics
- A less sophisticated approach can be followed by considering a series of common factors

When Quantitative Analysis Is Not Enough

- Quantitative data analysis has its limits and will likely need to be supplemented with qualitative data to complete the analysis process

Recommended Exercises:

1. Identify any material levels of change that may be evident within the current reporting period results.

2. Seek to identify cause and effect relationships that explain why those results occurred through analysis of quantitative data.

Chapter 9

Qualitative Data Analysis

Leveraging qualitative data to uncover the "why"

What Is Qualitative Data?

Qualitative Factors Explaining Cause and Effect

The User-Centric View

Applying Competitive Intelligence Insights

Other Qualitative Data Sources

Reaching Out to the Wider Organization

User Surveys

Relevant Forum Participation

What Is Qualitative Data?

Qualitative data is often distinguished by its expression in non-numeric terms. Within the world of web analytics, this distinction is less cut and dry as certain qualitative factors may have been derived from more quantitative means. For our purposes, we have separated out those factors that can be construed as being qualitative in nature and also included in this category, those insights that may have been derived from quantitative data resting outside of our own web site metric results.

As was mentioned in the last chapter, the application of qualitative data during analysis can serve to answer or explain why various performance results have occurred. They will be employed to supplement our quantitative data analysis to enhance understanding and complete any investigations where the numbers fell short of arriving at a solid answer. In addition, the discovery of a qualitative factor as a cause may in fact give rise to a need to collect new or return to existing quantitative data to support assertions or to test potential actions. The idea of taking action based on the assertions derived from analysis will be discussed in detail in a later chapter. For now, it is important to point out the interchangeable relationship that both qualitative and quantitative data share.

Qualitative Factors Explaining Cause and Effect

While reviewing analysis pertaining to quantitative data, the concept of cause and effect relationships was introduced as a means to simplify the effort to explain material changes or shifts within our current performance data. There, it was posited that any causes common to an individual web site prove to be rather subjective and relate directly to the differing nature of a particular web site and its offerings.

These varying and subjective factors will impact the type of user behavior exhibited across your web property and in turn, result in a set of potential causes common to your site but not necessarily universal in explanations employed elsewhere. For example, your site may undergo regular updates to its content, functions or architecture. Maybe, your site is more susceptible to various outside influences. This factor might include actions taken by different stakeholder groups within the organization or possible cultural or seasonal changes that lie outside of your control. During the early stages of our web analytics process formation, we did conduct exercises that should have provided some insight into more qualitative factors such as these. Review these documents again to sharpen your focus on what the causes are that may be occurring within your own web site to explain your current results.

By breaking down our analysis into simple cause and effect relationships, we put ourselves in a better position to arrive at conclusions that are easy to understand and straightforward to communicate to others. Taking this approach with at least a cursory understanding of what should and should not happen on our own site serves to sharpen this effort. The idea of adding more qualitative factors into the mix will serve to enhance one's ability to identify a cause and effect relationship and achieve a better understanding of performance results.

The User-Centric View

For further assistance in your cause analysis, we will first return to the concept of taking a user-centric view. In previous discussions, we mentioned this concept as a useful tool in understanding what user actions to measure, where they can be conducted and how to properly measure them. Here, we will look to apply this in the form of qualitative information to our search for specific causes explaining why a material change to one of our performance metrics has presented itself.

The first step taken after defining our objectives and goals was to map out the pages of the web site. One of the primary purposes of this act was to garner a better sense of how a visitor to the site might behave. When we reference taking a user-centric view, it means that we are putting ourselves into the shoes of a typical web site visitor and this early action was intended to foster this kind of perspective. In general terms, behavior is influenced by ones environment and the page map lays out the details of the setting our users are interacting within. We do not expect exact replication, psychic connection or anything of that nature to occur when seeking to employ this perspective. Instead, we hope to gain a different viewpoint that we can utilize in our analysis of the data and our search for causes.

Our metrics are tracking user actions across our site, from simple visits to more detailed direct actions and less concise but equally important interactions. Viewing these activities from the perspective of the ones' actually performing them will uncover more direct causes to explain the effects we are studying through web analytics.

To clarify this point, let's take a look at the following example. During analysis, a material change was uncovered relative to the KPI tracking the number of brochure downloads within the web site. The number and rate of these conversions remained unchanged against a measured increase in traffic across the web site over the same period. Further investigation did uncover a slight downward trend but no single event or site change could be uncovered to explain this occurrence. Using the page map as a starting place, a walkthrough of what steps a typical user might take in order to arrive at the point where downloads can occur first revealed that the link to perform the action was not easily found. Second, by following through on this exercise, the analyst realized that a user may not be comfortable providing all of the personal information asked of them before completing the download task.

These two new qualitative factors appeared to be the causes and prompted a return visit to the quantitative data for evidence to support the assertions. A deeper dive into the download details revealed that an increasing number of conversions were begun but not completed supporting the idea that an increasing aversion to providing personal information within the web site is occurring. The idea that the difficulty in finding the download link was a cause led to the construction of a test to try a new version to see if a positive impact on conversion results could be achieved.

Before moving on, we take a look at one more, brief example. Consider a web site tracking average time spent as a key performance indicator for one of its content sections. This particular metric often makes cause identification difficult as fluctuations measured within it can not be easily explained through quantitative means. Employing a user-centric view in a fashion similar to that found in the previous example is recommended as a first step. Time spent metrics relate directly to user interaction with available content. The more that is present, of interest and use to a typical user, the higher the time spent will be. If application of a user perspective fails to deliver clarity, investigating potential causes lying outside of your own web site's direct influence is advisable. Taking this additional step to see if industry, technology or cultural implications are at play will be addressed within the next section.

These examples demonstrate how a user-centric view can enhance the identification of a potential cause. Further, the application of such qualitative factors lead to additional quantitative data research, testing and can uncover a need for use of additional qualitative data sources. They also served to demonstrate the interchangeable relationship between these two data types. Again, subjectivity is a clear factor but the application of a user-centric view as a qualitative resource should be evident.

Applying Competitive Intelligence Insights

Competitive Intelligence was first cited as an alternative source for use in the development of baseline performance standards utilized in the measurement of our current data results. This resource can also serve as a repository of qualitative insights that can be applied to investigative analysis to explain metric fluctuations through cause and effect relationships. Competitive intelligence usage also stands as a prime example of web analytics data, expressed as qualitative insights that were derived from quantitative data resting outside of our web site specific information.

Its application within the web analytics analysis phase is not unlike what was described when employing a user-centric view. When initial quantitative analysis fails to uncover a cause for the current condition, insights derived from competitive intelligence research can be applied to directly answer the reason why or be used to facilitate additional quantitative investigation. Where these insights stand apart is their root in activity that lies outside of the realm of activity taking place directly on the web site. Competitive intelligence insights will consist of qualitative information pertaining to activity reflected in the competitive market and reflect more universal online performance and user behavior.

Another key difference relative to competitive intelligence is the need to generate these insights through a separate series of measurement and analysis steps. Your plate may already be pretty full and in light of this, we do not want to include an extensive series of competitive measurement and analysis steps to our regular web analytics process. While it would be great to know what quantitative trends are occurring outside of your own site, the collection and monitoring of this information could prove to strain existing resources. Instead, note the current traffic levels of the known competitors now using the tools listed in a previous chapter. When a need for this kind of insight arises later, a simple comparison of these documented traffic levels to relevant period competitor results can provide a basic indication of whether the market is trending up, down or remaining constant.

Accessing competitive intelligence tools for a wider array of insights can be performed in a simple fashion as well. A good indicator of current market results and behaviors can be gleaned from tools that track keyword usage and other search behavior both for competitors and the market in general. Social media behavior can be viewed as well. A list of some these tools that are currently available include the following:

Spyfu: Keywords your competitors are targeting

The Search Monitor: Tracks market share, page rank, ad copy, landing page, and even the budget of your competitors on paid and organic search

Compete Pro: In addition to more detailed competitive traffic data, it can also offer insights into search trends, historical search referral data, and filtering of the top performing keywords.

Postrank: Eases discovery of the most engaging blogs or what content is currently the hottest.

Google Insights: This tool lets you compare search volume patterns across several variables including filtering by category, seasonality and geography.

Web Page Readability: Maybe the reason why your competitor's web site is outperforming yours is because theirs is much more readable. This tool analyzes   the characteristics of a web site's writing using a multitude of readability scores. These insights can guide you in coming up with simpler, more effective content for your audience.

SM2: This software solution was designed for social media monitoring and measurement. With it, you can learn the gender, age, and location of who's talking; listen to what they're saying; assess their popularity or social media rankings; and find out where exactly the conversation is taking place.

There are sure to be other tools and services available to reference different aspects of competitor and general market activity to build qualitative insights that can be applied to your web analytics analysis as well.

Earlier, we mentioned the use of page maps to foster a user-centric view to assist in analysis efforts. We also noted the potential impact of site changes in both testing procedures and quantitative trend discovery. These can be referenced from an outside or competitive view using one of these tools:

Yahoo Site Explorer: Provides a map of competitor web sites.

Copernic Tracker: Monitors competitor web sites and notifies you of any changes.

Competitive Intelligence offers a rich array of resources to further identify causes within your own web site as we analyze results. We again want to emphasize that research in these areas can prove to be very useful but should not take away time and resources needed to monitor your own site.

Other Qualitative Data Sources

There are still other potential resources that can be tapped to provide an additional means to identify cause and effect relationships existing within our performance results. These alternatives will share characteristics that are similar both to the application of the user-centric view or the collection of insights from competitive intelligence sources. As such, the insights they deliver will be applied in the same fashion as shown in our most recent discussions.

Reaching Out to the Wider Organization

When quantitative data analysis has reached a dead-end, individuals and departments within the wider organization can be looped in to provide a new set of eyes in solving our cause identification problem. Earlier, it was noted that actions taken by another organizational team may impact online performance results. By sharing the results of your investigation with other organization members, the occurrence of these events or changes can be discovered. In turn, a deeper discussion regarding their nature and purpose could prove to produce the insight needed to tie an event or change back to the web analytics data as an explanation or cause. If technical or content related changes rest outside of your own control, reaching out to those individuals or departments that do implement them should become a common practice during the analysis phase of your process.

Other members of the organization can also serve as an alternative or supplement to any competitive intelligence gathering or research. While they may not have a strong digital background, their expertise in other aspects of an organization's operation may produce insights that are similar to what might be gleaned through more extensive research. Experienced individuals in sales, marketing, finance or other departments can also be employed to confirm any assertions made from research involving competitive analysis and other more, qualitative sources.

Digital metric analysis does not have to remain a "siloed" affair and its effectiveness can be increased by seeking additional insight and advice from others within the organization. Remember too that facilitating participation from individuals whose responsibilities lie outside of the immediate digital realm will serve to mitigate some of the challenges that could be encountered, as mentioned in the introduction of this book.

User Surveys

Understanding user behavior is a key focal point relative to our web analytics efforts. Insights into it can be derived from quantitative data, especially when derived from engagement type metrics. Utilizing a user perspective or tapping competitive and market research can supplement this understanding. However, user behavior is a somewhat ambiguous term and its understanding can be polluted by its inherent difficulty to measure and the subjectivity with which it can be expressed across different web sites.

In spite of this, shifts in user behavior can often serve as the cause discovered for material changes in our key performance metrics. This fact demands that such assertions relative to cause assignment must be made with at least some degree of accuracy or reliability in order to be effectively acted upon later. A solution to help fill the gap is the use of surveys as a means to improve understanding of our our web site's user behavior. If you want to know why certain actions or activities are taking place, who better to ask than those who are actually performing them? Just like when we reach internally within our organization, we look to the user base itself for additional insights that could be used to explain our current state of performance.

How we approach this external resource will dictate what kind of information is received. Asking a series of direct questions meant to explain why a user is not converting or has decreased visitation will ideally result in equally direct answers. Providing a means for users to share feedback on web site content or functions can result in a less direct, but more diverse collection of information that can be reviewed for additional insight. A survey of users can even serve a role in the testing of new applications, content or other changes that are being considered for implementation.

Regardless of the type of insights that may be needed, user surveys can be constructed to aid in many cause discovery processes. While their employment may not represent a consistent activity needed within the confines of your web analytics process, a series of options listed below can be employed to supplement your qualitative data resources:

>   User survey using a free tool (surveymonkey)

>   Email questions using your own user registry list

>   User feedback modules embedded within the web site

>   Real time pop-up surveys within the web site

Relevant Forum Participation

One final alternative resource for qualitative insights is the many digital marketing and web analytics forums currently active across the web. Analyzing web data is a pretty universal activity and is being performed by individuals with an array of backgrounds and experience. Performing a quick search on the Internet should result in many forum options that can be joined. Readers with a presence on Linkedin have a wide range of member groups available that foster discussion on common issues or serve as a resource to get specific questions answered.

Think of these relevant forums as a means to reach out to your external peers not unlike what was described with our other alternatives. You can participate directly in any discussions that might be occurring by asking questions or providing answers for others. You can still gather many useful insights simply by following along and reviewing any new topics for relevancy to your own analysis needs. Regardless, forums discussing topics relevant to web analytics, digital marketing or specific industry or web site types can provide a wealth of new information that can be applied in your own cause and effect data analysis.

Summary Outline

What Is Qualitative Data?

- For our purposes, qualitative data includes non-numeric information and any insights derived from quantitative measures resting outside of our own web site's metric results
- Quantitative and qualitative data share an interchangeable relationship relative to web analytics analysis efforts

Qualitative Factors Explaining Cause and Effect

- When quantitative data falls short, more qualitative sets of information can be applied to complete cause identification
- This need arises as a direct result of the subjectivity often in play when trying to decipher reasons why performance shifts have occurred

The User-Centric View

- Mentioned before as a useful tool in achieving better understanding relative to our goals, measurements and web site operation
- This perspective can be utilized to uncover potential causes in metric fluctuations

- Its use can foster the need for further quantitative analysis and testing or point to additional sources for new qualitative insights

Applying Competitive Intelligence Insights

- As a qualitative resource, insights gleaned from competitive research data can be applied to discover or explain causes during our own analysis
- Competitive data can cover traffic, search, market trends and user behavior
- The extent of information available can lead to dedication of too much valuable time and should be avoided
- Additional tools are listed to serve as resources to expand the degree and amount of insights that can be gleaned

Other Qualitative Data Sources

- A further set of alternatives is available to tap for insight as we analyze our performance results
- Reaching out to individuals or departments within the wider organization
- Conducting user surveys or reviewing web site feedback
- Participating in relevant forum discussions

Recommended Exercises:

1. Continue to perform cause and effect analysis using qualitative data to complete any unresolved investigations.

Chapter 10
Taking Action
Converting our insights into actions and policies

Overview

Actionable Insights

The Action Plan

Best Practices

Overview

To this point, a lot has been accomplished. Thus far, we have established specific objectives and goals for our site, identified key performance metrics, collected and measured our data and analyzed our results through both quantitative and qualitative means. The product of all of this effort is a series of insights that established, through cause and effect relationship discovery, explanations as to why our performance is in its current state.

What comes next is to take these newly discovered insights and convert them into direct actions that will reverse any negative trends and ensure continuation of actions or events that resulted in positive ones.

Actionable Insights

Our step by step approach had led us to a point where we are able to analyze our web property's traffic data to measure performance and gain insight into the various causes that affect it. Achieving this level of understanding is a primary focus of web analytics but it means little unless this new knowledge can be applied to influence our future operation.

If you have not done so already, write down the various insights (cause and effect relationships) that your recent analysis has uncovered. Revisit each and assign a specific action that can be taken to improve your web site's performance. When dealing with positive performance results, write down what action, event or circumstance most contributed to this outcome. Each insight uncovered during our analysis must have the ability to convert into an actionable item or contribute to your future performance in the form of a best practice. If you encounter difficulty with this exercise, it is recommended that you review your previous analysis to see if the original insights do, in fact, represent a true cause and effect relationship. When they do, the resulting "effect" provides a call to action that can be followed through to reverse or maintain its course.

Actionable insights derived from negative outcomes should be addressed as soon as possible. When formulating a response to them, consider what can be accomplished in the short term to immediately affect their direction. For example, when a negative conversion trend is determined to have been caused by a combination of decreased traffic and a perceived difficulty for a user to complete the action, decide on steps that can increase overall traffic and seek a means to alter the positioning, path or presence of the conversion point within the web site. To clarify, traffic can be increased by adjusting the current or starting a new web traffic campaign through search, social media or digital banners. Easing users' ability to complete a conversion task can be addressed by reducing the number of pages or clicks needed within the web site to arrive at the point of action. Further, the information required from a user can be altered or limited if that was the issue causing the downward shift. The actions chosen in the short term will vary depending on the cause and the resources that are currently available. As in the example above, when multiple causes are in play, at least some should offer an opportunity to take immediate action. Those that do not should be added to an action list and followed through upon as soon as you are able.

Actionable insight derived from positive outcomes, which now can be referred to as our best practices, should also be implemented in the short term where needed. Some best practices discovered through the analysis process will represent actions or circumstances that have already been enacted. These can be reviewed to see if their application can prove useful in any other areas. For example, consider the discovery of a best practice derived from a highly successful article published on the web site and posted to a Facebook page as well. The article itself used a humor spin to express ideas around a currently hot topic uncovered during previous market research efforts. Its success was expressed in the high degree of engagement it received within the web site through higher than average unique visitors and average time spent. The article's posting on Facebook also served to out perform other content by its larger-than-average traffic contribution to the web site.

This discovery led to the documentation of a best practice where humor was cited as a means to increase article readership. It also noted the need to post popular articles within the organization's Facebook page in an effort to drive more significant levels of traffic. Finally, it confirmed the value of market research in discovering which topics can generate the most interest from users. Three distinct, but interrelated practices were pulled from a single discovery in this case. Immediate action can be taken here by reviewing other articles to ensure that the most popular ones to date have been employed to drive traffic through an additional social media posting. Further, the practice of conducting some initial research to learn what the best topics might be for the next piece can be communicated to those responsible for content management. If all of these options have already been enacted prior to this discovery, the confirmation of their success can be shared to encourage continuation of the best practice.

Insights derived from positive or negative outcomes are united by their ability to exert influence on our future web site performance. As was demonstrated in the previous examples, some insights will offer more immediate options with which to take action and some may already be enacted. Regardless, we utilize our collection of insights to create a plan of action that can be implemented to alter our course or ensure that it continues along a positive path.

The Action Plan

We now look to document our new collection of direct actions in the form of a list that can be referenced for future follow up. It was earlier recommended to follow through with a sense of immediacy. Realistically, this will not always be possible and a list detailing all of the actions decided upon can serve as a checklist to track progress in getting them completed.

When creating this document, it may even make sense to note some of the logic behind each item's inclusion by associating its original cause. The examples from the last section provided options that could be acted upon in the short term. However, upon more reflection, it may be determined that implementing a new campaign utilizing search or other media will require some thought before its execution. Citing the need to adjust the setting or access of a conversion point can also create a need for additional thought, analysis or testing as the list of potential opportunities could be quite extensive. Further, any implementation may call for the addition of other resources and inclusion could have numerous repercussions.

As in this case, this new action list could contain items whose implementation would benefit from further interaction and discussion with others within the wider organization. They may also foster a need to collect the advice and opinions of peers or web site users. In circumstances like these, the action plan can serve to facilitate needed communication with others and be used to guide discussions to a more meaningful result.

Focus For the Next Reporting Period

Another valuable use for the action plan can be found as you begin the measurement and analysis process for the next reporting period. All of the direct actions initiated from the prior term will serve as the first items of focus in the next. While each of them was decided upon using solid and sometimes extensive measurement and analysis, they were still based on assertions using only the information at hand. It is possible that they do not garner the results expected in the next period indicating that our assertions were incorrect or that additional analysis is needed.

The dynamism inherent within the Internet itself prevents any absolute guarantee that any single or series of actions will always work. In this light, all actions that are implemented need to be reviewed in the next reporting period to either confirm their success or derive a new or adjusted action to take in an effort to improve performance. In many cases too, this confirmation will not be met until a series of subsequent reporting period results have passed and the new trend intended from the intervention has been established.

To Illustrate, let's look at another example. Consider a web site whose product sale conversion rate had dropped consistently for the last several months. Analysis insight led to an action that lowered the price of two specific items accounting for most of the conversion rate decline. The next reporting period showed a slight increase in the sale of each of these newly priced products. The action item performed was then crossed off the list as the issue appeared to have been corrected. The conversion metric did not show any material levels of change in the next couple analysis sessions and was not given attention, even though one or more had actually fallen a bit. Several months later, the same two products were discovered as the cause for yet another significant drop in overall conversions leading to a realization that the action taken so long ago had not really corrected the issue after all. Price helped in the short term but the products in question had become quite obsolete, even back then and that was the real cause for the drop in sales.

So what does this example tell us? First, it would have been wise to continue monitoring the results of the conversion rate in question beyond just a single month. The added attention may have prompted a more thorough follow up review that could have discovered the real reason for the sales shift at a much earlier date. Even if an actual negative trend was not readily apparent, continued monitoring of results would have been justified until a greater degree of comfort in the action's success was established.

This also could have an impact in a more indirect sense. A premature confirmation might lead to further application of the same action to resolve similar issues arising in later reporting periods. If this happened as well, the original issue would not only reappear, but may have also been multiplied with far larger shifts in overall performance results. As you can see, the impact of actions taken on behalf of our analysis insights goes beyond metric results as they have the potential to transform into more common practices themselves.

Action's Influence

We just presented the idea that those actions that have been implemented to alter web site performance have the potential to exert influence beyond those items that they were meant to specifically address. As we continue to make assertions and take action, those resulting in success can and likely will be reapplied when similar situations arise. Each confirmed success adds to our understanding of the web site's operation and improves our ability to identify and eventually eliminate common causes and their resulting effects. In essence, earlier actions can become new best practices if their confirmed success and future application dictates.

While this certainly highlights the importance of confirming the results of our actions, it also illuminates the continued opportunity to generate an even greater degree of insight after initial discovery. Again we are confronted with the dynamism of the web analytics process and the interrelationships present amongst each of its various steps. Insight leads to action which in turn leads to further monitoring and the creation of new, more universal insights that enhance our ability and overall experience.

Best Practices

The action plan centers on activity meant to influence the negative outcomes discovered during analysis. Best practices also should be documented in a separate list to meet a similar purpose. Like our direct actions, best practices require confirmation to ensure that our assertions are indeed correct. Best practices are intended to reflect what is being done right relative to the operation of our web site and we do want to ensure that this is the case. However, they do represent a more persistent assertion in contrast to those associated with direct action and do not necessarily lend themselves to true confirmation after a few subsequent reporting periods.

It can be argued that only through continuous, regular monitoring of results that assurance of their effectiveness is provided. One drop off within results influenced by the best practice can raise concerns if not nullify it outright. In the real world, this can occur but does it really call our earlier assertion into question? We certainly have plenty to occupy our attention without having to watch those areas we already deemed to be succeeding. In lieu of this fact, it is not recommended that a commitment be made to watch results related to any best practice ad infinitum. We should not be worrying about what is going right with our web site when we should be more focused on what might be wrong. Instead, we utilize this list of best practices as a supplemental tool for use in our future analysis efforts. Their confirmation is not grounded in the subsequent tracking of results thought to be directly derived from them. We will attempt to express how this authentication can be arrived at next.

Confirming Best Practices

Recall the example that cited the need to continue posting the best articles to the organization's Facebook page as a means to drive traffic. This represented a new best practice that could be continued on a persistent basis to take advantage of the additional traffic this policy has shown to provide. Not monitoring all future article traffic driving results does not call this new practice into question. The logic for its use is sound. Any fluctuations down the road are more attributable to the article choice rather than the act of posting to Facebook itself.

Recall also that this example described articles with a humorous take on current, hot topics as being the best options to drive traffic. The specificity implied in this example tells us that the choice made relative to article type or content does impact the final performance result of the newly proposed practice. We may now be in a better position to argue a more consistent need to monitor results as we have no guarantees that humorous slants will always be the best options when choosing articles. We also do not know if their effectiveness will ever justify removal of them from our repertoire either.

So where does this example leave us relative to the question of confirming our best practices? First, it highlights the fact that a specific event or occurrence can be broken apart to reveal a higher level of practice that can be followed. Posting an article to Facebook serves as an instance. As we get more specific, the potential for more volatility relative to the continuation of positive results can be ascertained through simple application of logic or common sense. The test to apply here is to simply ask yourself how many factors could influence the continued positive outcome in the future? Posting an article to Facebook had one clear factor; the choice of the article. The use of articles with a humorous slant has to account for topic relevancy, current and future user tastes, writing ability and so on. A best practice should reflect a higher level of operation and avoid too much specificity in order to be effective.

Rather than tracking results to confirm the authenticity or reliability of our discovered best practices, we instead have looked at their make-up itself, and ensured that a more stable policy unencumbered with too many specific criteria has emerged. By documenting our newly discovered best practices in a list, we can review their logic and adjust them to reflect a higher level of action that will prove to be less volatile and consequently, less likely to require continuous monitoring for confirmation. As with the action plan, the original assertions (cause and effect relationships) discovered to create them can be included to better facilitate this review and confirm our new policies.

Likewise, a best practice can also be confirmed through its application as we move forward to subsequent reporting periods. Understanding that posting of articles to Facebook is a good practice immediately will call attention to an article itself when analysis uncovers a correlation to a metric shift. Further, when more traffic is needed to correct a particular conversion downturn, it is known that articles posted to Facebook can be utilized in some way to impact this. In one case, the best practice served to narrow focus to a lower level issue. In the other, it provided a ready made answer to a new issue.

Revisiting the Action Plan

Return again to the action plan created to document the direct actions chosen to influence our performance results. At the end of its discussion, it was posited that their confirmation represented the foundation of a new insight that could be applied in future analysis efforts. As their effectiveness is confirmed and they are progressively applied to resolve future cause and effect relationships, these actionable insights begin to take on the characteristics found in our best practices.

In a previous example, we cited a situation where an action was taken to address a decrease in sales conversions relative to two specific products. Their price was dropped but the resulting increase in sales resulted in what was later determined to be only a temporary fix. Eventually, the product offerings themselves proved to be the problem as they were already in need of replacement due to the products' obsolescence. The lesson derived from that example related to the need to properly confirm an action's success and avoid compounding issues through subsequent use. Here we can still see how this example can lead to a new set of best practices by looking a bit further down the road.

After discovery of the real issue causing the drop in sales, price change was used as a temporary measure to forestall the need for new products. Knowing this, research was conducted immediately after the implementation of a price drop to identify new product replacements to better meet current user purchase desires. As we can see, two potentially new policies have emerged. First, a price decrease appears to be an effective means to extend the life of an obsolete product while a replacement is sought. Second, when sales begin a downward decline, a signal surfaces indicating that the product may no longer be generating consumer interest or meeting current needs. This signal prompts a search for a new product replacement. What this illustrates is the existence of a cycle where an action leads to an insight which prompts yet another action that generates an improved level of insight.

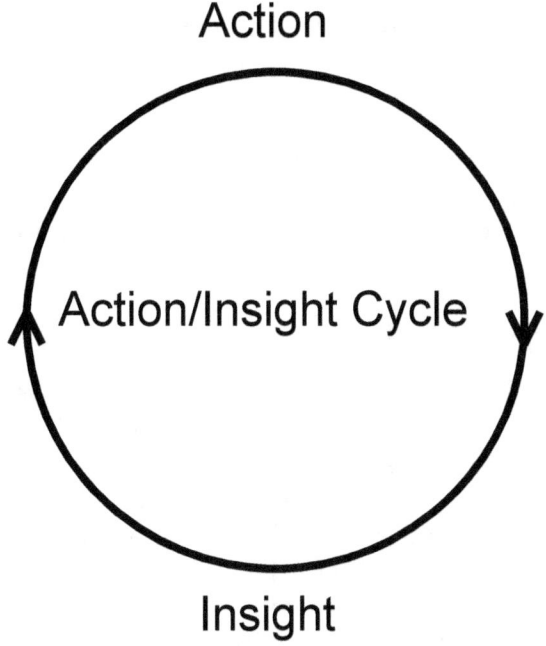

Exhibit 2: The Action/Insight Cycle

Eventually, the confirmed success of the action will lead to its use to resolve other, similar problems that arise during performance result analysis. Such continued application can confirm this direct response as a new best practice policy that can be incorporated into the web analytics "toolbox" as a common response to issues arising relative to falling product sales. Even though its discovery was derived from two very specific products, continued application implies that this particular action ignores that level of specificity and represents a higher level policy that is unencumbered by product characteristics.

What also gets demonstrated is the idea that such insights can be discovered equally through failures as much as they can through success. Remember, in the original example, the use of price adjustment later proved to be incorrect at least in terms of providing a long-term "cause-generated" solution. Its premature confirmation did not prevent the emergence of more improved insight and the eventual creation of an effective new policy. As is shown in exhibit 2, the cyclical nature of actions and insights foster this kind of discovery even in the wake of mistakes or delays.

With this understanding established, we can now look to our action plan as another source of new best practices. As these direct actions are confirmed they can be crossed off the list but now we can also look to add them to our set of best practices and utilize them in future analysis processes.

Learning and Improvement

Like so many other aspects of the web analytics process, we can never truly say that there is a list of best practices for all to follow and that there effective application is truly permanent. Regardless of how we arrive at their establishment as policies to follow within our own web analytics process, we resolve ourselves to the fact that what they represent is our most recent set of learnings that can be employed to better improve current and future results. This concept ties us directly back to the original uses of our selected key performance indicators making a best practice's creation and use a validation of their worth.

Summary Outline

Overview

- All of the work accomplished to this point has led us to the need to convert insights discovered during analysis into action

Actionable Insights

- Assign a specific action that can influence performance to each newly discovered cause and effect relationship
- Actions designed to reverse negative outcomes should be implemented immediately
- Events or circumstances that explain positive outcomes should be documented as future best practices

- A properly formed cause and effect relationship will allow for the conversion of an insight into something that is actionable

The Action Plan

- Document newly assigned, direct actions into a list or plan of action
- Immediate implementation is often not possible creating a need for an action item list that can monitor progress
- The action plan can also serve as a reminder relative to what items should be focused on in the next analysis session
- After implementation, each action and the performance results they were intended to modify need to be reviewed to confirm success
- Confirmation should be derived from the establishment of a new, positive trend
- A lack of confirmation will lead to additional analysis until a suitable solution is discovered
- Successful actions can wield influence beyond the short term in the form of future application to similar cause and effect relationships

Best Practices

- Explanations of positive outcomes should be documented in another list comprising of best practices
- Continual tracking of results could be argued in order to confirm best practices but this is not recommended
- Breaking them down and removing any specificity should result in a higher level policy with few factors that foster volatility in results
- Best practices are confirmed through their successful application in other, similar circumstances
- The best practice list serves as a means to review insights and convert them into policies that can be implemented in future analysis sessions
- The action plan can be revisited and those actions proved to be effective can be moved to the best practice list
- Taking action and deriving insight is a cyclical process that will eventually lead to the formation of new best practices
- Best practices function as documented representations of our most current learnings

Recommended Exercises:

1. Review all newly discovered cause and effect relationships and convert insights into actionable items. When none can be derived, review your original assertions as some action or best practice should be produced.

2. Document all actions and best practices in a list.

3. Document and review each best practice in order to reflect a more high level policy.

4. Add newly confirmed successful actions to the best practices list in the form of new, high level policies.

Chapter 11

Web Strategy Formation

Employing actions and policies to form a comprehensive web strategy

Web Strategy

Insights, Actions and Policies

Site Optimization

Search Engine Optimization

Search Engine Marketing

Display Advertising

Traditional Advertising And Other External Influences

User Experience

Resource Allocation

Site Monetization

Long-Term Strategy Communication

Web Strategy

A strategy can be defined as a plan of action designed to achieve a specific vision. Successful organizations of all sizes employ some form of strategy that provides the direction to follow in order to achieve a "vision" defined through their overall goals. A web strategy does the same but relates only to an organization's web site or other digital operations. It too offers a framework to follow in order to achieve associated goals and objectives and can outline web positioning, preferred user experience, branding, engagement methods and traffic conversion into sales.

Immediately, you can recognize the role of your own objectives and goals as they serve to provide your intended vision. Each was documented and defined based on the original intent of your web site and represented only the most important aspects of operation that would be measured and analyzed to foster better performance. Each subsequent step performed throughout the web analytics process was driven by these initial goals and led to a series of actionable insights meant to improve results and optimize performance. What is clear is that a vision comprised of the most fundamental and important intentions drove a need to measure and analyze results until the best possible outcomes could be achieved through the derived actions and best practices.

As we took these first steps into the world of web analytics, we also were forming the foundation of a web strategy by defining a vision and further uncovering the actions and policies needed to achieve its maximum result. Not unlike the opening of the chapter on measurement, many of the steps needed to formulate a comprehensive course of direction have been done. Our next set of topics will seek to consolidate your understanding of this and demonstrate how the different steps of the web analytics process contribute to the beginnings of a web strategy.

Insights, Actions and Policies

Strategy is often viewed as a more long-term plan of action and this is certainly true. However, it was stated earlier that our actionable insights leading to direct, immediate actions help to form the basis of our web strategy. On the surface, this does not jive but again consider the notion

John Cassidy Jr.

that these actions can have a significant impact on our future performance. Let's say, you encountered a negative trend relative to a content page's average time spent. You determined that the content was out-of-date and users' interest in reading the various articles presented had waned. You noted that the action needed to reverse this trend was to upload new content. You took a direct action with the intent to reverse a negative trend in the near term. However, this particular example does lend itself to becoming a more long-term, best practice similar to examples employed in the last chapter. After further reflection, you realize that if new content is not uploaded on a regular basis, it is very likely that the negative results you uncovered now could return in the future. What was intended to influence performance in the short term actually proved to be a solution requiring implementation over the long term. It can be argued that this immediate, direct action actually represented a change in operating policy that will impact performance on an ongoing basis into the future. For the sake of expediency we will presume that this new policy has been confirmed and characterized in such a manner to allow its label as a best practice.

So far, we have detailed an example that is similar in all respects (save for its use of assumption) to those provided earlier in our discussions on the cycle moving from insight to action until a true best practice is arrived at. It is at this point that we make the leap to web strategy formation using the best practice as the building block. The new policy created to encourage regular updates to the web site's content provides a step to be completed to move further in the direction toward the fulfillment of the site's original vision.

The key performance indicator related to user engagement of content was analyzed to eventually reach the conclusion that this policy was needed on a regular basis. The KPI itself was assigned as a means to measure the performance of a web site goal and objective derived from the reasons for which it was originally created. In this way, the newly created policy can be linked back to the web site's original vision and serve as part of the direction defined within its own web strategy.

Again, we have demonstrated how an insight turns into a direct action and eventually can transform into a best practice. We have now taken it one step further and established its place as part of a developing web strategy meant to guide our efforts toward the maximization of performance relative to our original objectives and goals. The best practice list and to a certain degree, the action plan, that we created earlier can now be viewed as the blueprint of a web strategy as it can give us the kind of steps needed to ensure that our efforts are being guided in the correct direction.

Site Optimization

We have defined web strategy rather broadly to this point. From our earlier efforts, we have a running list of regular actions and practices that combine to form an "operational blueprint" relative to our web site's performance future. We can further characterize this as our collection of practices, tools or techniques employed to optimize our web site. In other words, this list details or defines our site optimization strategy.

Site optimization is commonly referred to as the effort to maximize performance through optimal site architecture and effective and efficient resource usage. You are probably very familiar with the term Search Engine Optimization or SEO and we would consider this to be a large part of any site optimization effort. We classify actions and practices using the broader term because many site optimization efforts are not necessarily correlated directly with search. Examples of these would include actions or practices enacted to improve user experience or organization resource allocation relative to web site operation. Other digital advertising options are available to be employed within traffic driving campaigns as well. We can also distinguish between SEO and its cousin, search engine marketing or SEM as distinct contributors to web site optimization.

Site optimization represents the intent of all of our web analytics efforts and is interchangeable with any definition of a web strategy. As strategy is developed to achieve a pre-defined vision for an organization, so does site optimization as it focuses on reaching the optimal level of performance relative to a web site's objectives and goals. As you look back upon your lists of actions and best practices, you can better understand their place within the formation of a more comprehensive web or site optimization strategy by taking a closer look at the components most commonly associated with generating optimal web site performance.

Before we dive in, please note that many of these proceeding topics are extensive enough to serve as the subject of their own books. Many such resources are available and provide a great deal of detail relative to their definition, use and implementation. We will only conduct a very high level discussion for each here but it is encouraged to seek other supporting resources to supplement your own understanding as needed.

In addition, all of the components of site monetization briefly discussed below may already be represented within your current plan of action or list of best practices. Their descriptions are intended to foster a better understanding of site optimization and the various aspects that may contribute to its accomplishment. Each component shares the same end, maximization or optimization of performance relative to a web site's objectives and goals (its pre-defined vision).

Search Engine Optimization

Search Engine Optimization is the process of making a web site or a particular web page more visible through organic or un-paid search results. In general, focus is placed on achieving a higher rank and more frequent appearance in relevant search inquiries. This is already well-known and was likely at the forefront of your mind when you first began this process.

As a component of our budding web strategy, we tie search engine optimization into web analytics through its use as a potential action to address insights uncovered during our analysis. Many of the cause and effect relationships we identify will dictate actions or culminate in best practice policies that involve manipulation or maintenance of our current web site traffic. Remember the previous example detailing the action arrived at to reverse a drop in average time spent? Our solution in this hypothetical scenario was to upload new content to re-invigorate user engagement on the web site. This action and the subsequent policy established to perform regular content uploads serves as a means to optimize organic search engine results by better aligning site content with what users are looking for across the web. Keep in mind that this did not involve implementing or increasing advertising spend but instead dealt only with the alteration of the web site itself.

This fact is what distinguishes search engine optimization from other traffic driving efforts as it is meant to affect the site's own traffic generation ability without the use of supporting advertising campaigns.

Search engine optimization can also take the form of article distribution as a means to drive organic traffic. Whether they are written specifically for this purpose or chosen from pre-existing web site content, article copy can be optimized like web site pages to foster a higher degree of search results and subsequent click-throughs. Articles utilized in this fashion can be published within supplemental blogs or other social media pages and tools to encourage users to seek out the main web site for similar or more enhanced content. Several options are also available to foster a wider range of distribution through content publication on other, external web sites and blogs. Further investigation conducted outside of the scope of this book will reveal a whole set of techniques built around such a traffic driving concept.

Search Engine Marketing

Search engine marketing or SEM can be distinguished from search engine optimization simply by the fact that it seeks to manipulate or maintain web traffic through execution of search advertising activities. Unlike search engine optimization, SEM is made up primarily of paid traffic generation in the form of keyword selection and bidding to improve a site's rank as users search for information or functions that meet their needs.

Perfecting its use relative to your own web site can involve a great deal of time and practice and can be performed on a spot basis or along more continuous lines. In this light, it can transform from a specific, direct action into a more permanent and universal policy or set of policies to be enacted as a means to maximize web site performance. Within the web analytics process, the results of a search engine marketing campaign can be tracked as a separate entity unto itself or through its impact relative to key performance indicators of the web site.

Display Advertising

It is assumed that many, if not all, readers of this book are just getting started with web analytics. As such, it is entirely likely that your initial traffic driving activities will likely not stray beyond organic and paid search applications. However, there are other traffic driving options available that can be integrated into your web strategy. The most common form of digital advertising outside of search is the banner ad. These come in a variety of shapes and sizes and can be placed across the full array of web site types. Use in certain social media offerings and within mobile applications is also common. Like SEO and SEM, use of banner ads will be driven by the insights and related actions and practices derived from our analysis. Similar to search engine related activities, the application of these various advertising methods can consist of one time or continuous campaigns meant to reflect direct action or policy implementation respectively. Where the use of banner or display ads begins to differ is in how web analytics is used to inform in decisions related to their implementation.

As already mentioned, search engine marketing involves a bid process where you pay a pre-determined amount for your end-result, a click. Display advertising also shares the same end-result but you instead pay for impressions with the expectation that clicks to your site will follow. This is the first point of departure from search related efforts. Second, traffic analysis conducted as part of your web analytics process can be utilized to assess the potential benefit of different advertising options and weigh them against their expected cost. For example, if your average conversion rate for a particular action is 5% against all traffic to your site, you can surmise through an expected click estimate how much more traffic an ad might bring and further calculate what impact this has on your straight conversion count and subsequent revenue. With search marketing, you will already know the cost per click before moving forward and can conduct the same comparison much more quickly. With banner ads, a bit more work is required and a good deal more estimation is involved.

Web sites dedicated to the sale of similar advertising options often will still employ these types of efforts but supplement the use of web analytics analysis with an assessment of the return on investment relative to their own sale of ad space. Ad campaigns undertaken to increase one's own impression inventory are justified if the expense generated by the additional impressions is outweighed by an increase in expected ad space revenue. Revisit the earlier discussion on the assignment of economic value and ROI if clarification is needed.

Traditional Advertising and Other External Influences

In addition to the most common digital options, one must not overlook the potential influence of other, non-digital marketing activities. First, the placement of ads can range across more traditional mediums like TV, radio and print. Unification of digital and traditional mediums within advertising campaigns has become much more common today and has done much to eliminate the "siloeing" present in organizations that was previously mentioned as a potential challenge relative to web analytics. Many readers may not expand their traffic driving efforts into more traditional advertising mediums but they deserve mention here for the potential influence they can have. Traditional media campaigns that do not incorporate digital assets or web site mentions can still influence site performance indirectly and insight related to this relationship can emerge through qualitative data gathering discussions facilitated internally.

Mention of this here serves to call out the idea that some insights may not be directly reflected within our current direct actions or policies but may instead be the driving force behind their creation or practice. This fact accentuates the need to document the logic behind chosen actions and practices so that their implementation as a part of a site optimization strategy is fully understood.

Performance influence can also be derived from actions taken by other departments and stakeholders of your web site like marketing, legal and sales. Traditional media campaigns managed elsewhere in the organization could be counted as a potential example. In addition, cultural and technological influences can prove to impact your web site's traffic performance and can be accounted for within your wider site optimization strategy.

In the earlier discussions on data analysis we did note that such external forces could supply the cause for the particular effect you are investigating. In that phase, we encouraged looking beyond areas of your own direct control for answers and we reiterate that sentiment here. Qualitative data derived from market or competitive research, internal discussions or external peer or user interaction can serve to uncover previously unknown, external influences. When such influences are made apparent through careful analysis, their role within a site optimization strategy is likely to mirror that described with influences fostered from traditional media. They likely are the driving force behind various digital actions or policies enacted to mitigate or encourage their influences.

User Experience

Another component of our web strategy centers on the user experience provided within a web site. This strategic aspect will often overlap with other components as it directly affects the environment in which our site visitors interact. We separate it out from because of the emphasis it demands relative to its enormous impact.

We define user experience as the way an individual feels about interacting with our web property and its offerings. User experience highlights the experiential aspects of a visitor's interaction with our site and also includes their perception of utility, ease of use and efficiency within our property's system. Like many other aspects of a site optimization strategy and the supporting web analytics, user experience is dynamic in nature and experiences change over time.

Cause and effect relationships identified through our analysis will often uncover issues that can be classified as relating to the user experience. We can refer back to a previous hypothetical example that detailed the affect of poor navigation on the sales of a particular product. Recall the action taken from that insight involved alteration of the site's existing navigation architecture. This was done to improve users' ability to locate the product in question thereby improving their perception of the web site's ease of use. This example differs from an SEO activity in the fact that the intended result did not involve ease of discovery from a search engine point of view. The change was derived from a need to improve onsite user experience and likely would not have any direct affect on search engine results. These kinds of changes can overlap with search engine optimization efforts under certain circumstance but, as already mentioned, they would still qualify as a means to a similar end. While such an example illustrates an action that directly impacts the user experience of the web site, it also contributes to site optimization by uncovering a potentially common issue and accompanying solution that can be referenced in future analysis procedures.

Whenever we determine that causes of metric fluctuation are derived directly from the existing state of our web site's navigation, page layout, content or functionality, we can classify it as pertaining to user experience. Of course, you may realize that many of these issues can also relate to the web site's traffic and may have been altered originally to impact this. In many cases this is in fact true and again supports our earlier assertion that user experience does overlap with other components of our strategy. What you need to come away with however, is the idea that issues concerning your web site's user experience are highly important, do in fact overlap in their impact with many of our other efforts and represent a focus on site optimization in its purest form. A focus on improving the user experience will lead to an optimal site architecture that provides visitors the information and functionality they seek in the most efficient manner possible.

Resource Allocation

We have described site optimization generally as an effort to improve the efficiency of our web site's operation. That need for optimal efficiency goes beyond the web site itself to include the various organizational resources employed to make it run. So why is this part of our discussion concerning site optimization strategy?

To answer this, let's step back and take stock of what we have discussed thus far. From the very beginning, the need to focus our web analytics efforts around the most important goals and their related measurement metrics has been emphasized. We have also sought to simplify the analysis of our data through consistent organization and basic cause and effect relationships. All of this discussion has been centered on maximizing one of the web site's primary resources; namely you.

However, here we are looking beyond the immediate to point out where application of web analytics can lead to better efficiency in resource allocation and in turn, be integrated into an ongoing site optimization strategy. To make this connection, return to the example described during our discussion on digital advertising. In that scenario, we detailed how web analytics plays a role in the decision to employ different media campaigns through analysis of the costs and benefits or ROI. Unlike search campaigns, digital and mobile media advertising requires estimation of desired results in order to predict the associated benefits that said campaigns may provide. This example relates to the efficient allocation of resources by using the cost benefit analysis to determine whether to move forward or not. In other words, it demonstrates an example of managing the allocation of a resource; the advertising budget.

We incorporate these types of efforts into our site optimization strategy in a similar fashion to the one described when building and comparing current metrics to historical data. Each time we perform an assessment that directly impacts the allocation of a resource; we need to focus on building a baseline result that we can easily compare to in the future. Over time, we will collect live results from our ad efforts, solidify our means of assessing their benefits compared to costs and attain greater efficiency in the allocation of our resource.

The digital advertising example lends itself well to the explanation of this concept but other types of resources and their allocation can be impacted in the same way. Let's take a look at your web site's technical support resources. You may perform updates to the site yourself, have a supporting IT department or a third party vendor to rely on. Costs associated with each of these could range from allocation of simple time to regular or even significant monetary expense. Regardless, we should seek the most efficient allocation of our given resource in this case and can utilize the cost/benefit analysis and the formation of baselines to establish guiding principles that can be referred to for future use. If an actionable insight, uncovered during your analysis dictated that a change to one of your existing web pages be made, you would be wise to first confirm that this effort and its associated cost be worthy of the subsequent benefit you would receive; the reversal or prevention of the original cause that was uncovered. Referring again to the assignment of economic value can be useful here.

Web sites differ vastly in their nature and offerings and do not always lend themselves so directly to the cost benefit analysis described above. Even so, the allocation of any related resource, including your own time and attention should be done so in a manner that ensures its most efficient use. Keep this concept in mind as you formulate actionable insights and incorporate the baselines of your decision making into your overall site optimization strategy.

Site Monetization

The last area we will touch on relative to site optimization is the monetization of the web property itself. We define site monetization simply as the effort to maximize the amount of revenue that can be generated from the digital property. This component will not apply to all sites and will likely pertain to those offering products for sale, affiliate links or ad space for paying clients. Again we are confronted with a topic that can command a great deal of discussion in its own right. We will touch on some of the more basic aspects of site monetization to demonstrate its role in the formation of our site optimization strategy.

Site monetization is not unlike the other components of site optimization. You simply substitute in revenue or currency as the primary end we seek through our efforts. In fact, actions, practices and policies enacted to increase site revenue are the very same we have discussed within other components of site optimization. The most basic response to a drop in the number of actual sales is to increase the traffic driven to the page or pages that contribute to an online sale. Like before these type of actions can be added to our repertoire of tools found within our overall site optimization strategy to maintain and grow our desired performance metrics.

Where we differ from previous discussions is the idea that new monetization efforts can be derived from web analytics efforts that did not exist previously. The current objectives and goals of the site may not include such revenue generating focus today but they may tomorrow. Also, those sites that do sell products or ad space will likely be presented with opportunities to evolve their offerings in ways that were not originally conceived. It is this distinction that we wish to call your attention in terms of formulating your web strategy as an extension of your current analysis.

To illustrate, let's look at another example. Say your analysis dictated a necessity to upload more current content on a regular basis that more closely aligns with user needs, similar to a previous scenario. Instead, factor in the detail that you also sell ad space and a drop in the number of views of client banner ads was the effect driving your search for a cause and a subsequent solution. Later analysis proves that this act achieved the desired outcome in the form of recovery of former levels of ad engagement. Let us also include the fact that your site's ad space was designed to take advantage of the type of target audience that typically consumes such content and in-turn, attracts a specific class of advertiser clients.

With all of these facts in play, what impact is made on our strategy formation that distinguishes more specific, site monetization type decisions and efforts? Well, we can go in two directions, both of which, as you will see, warrant a separate discussion from those found earlier in this chapter. First, later analysis of our results may reveal no further growth in our recently influenced results or may have begun to decline. Our search for a cause must go beyond our original assertion as some other factor is at work. After review of current audience segments and their various dimensions, it is realized that a shift has occurred that was brought on by the recently implemented policy of uploading more, currently relevant content. This act has begun to attract a different audience segment than the one that is responding to the current advertisers' messaging. So what do we make of this development? Assuming the presence of this new segment is consistent, we either have to shift the overall focus of our ad space offering to a new client base or think about adding to that existing base, clients and messaging that better aligns with the new audience segment. Granted, this demonstrates a more complicated hypothetical setting than the ones previously explored but all of our basic tools and means to reach new conclusions remain at work.

The second direction offers a more indirect means to apply the site monetization concept to our web strategy. Here, we instead look at our overall site, its pages, content, functions and offerings and look for new opportunities before occurrences, like the one just detailed, arise. We incorporate certain guidelines into our ongoing site optimization strategy that will serve to call attention to potential, future revenue opportunities through more detailed audience monitoring. Also, we do the same relative to the dynamic qualities of our content and functional offerings. As they change or evolve, so may our audience. As we add new categories or distinctive offerings, so goes the addition of potential new revenue generating options that we have at our disposal.

Again, a good deal of discussion can be had around this topic and we want to remain focused on "getting started" in web analytics versus tackling more and more complicated questions, topics and issues. However, as with all aspects of our web analytics discussion, time and experience will prove to open these doors more widely driving the complicated more toward the trivial. Remember, it is our intent to build a strong foundation that will be built upon increasingly and awareness of these types of considerations work to serve that purpose.

Long-Term Strategy Communication

Strategy's very definition implies that it is long-term in nature. As we looked at the various components of site optimization we were able to better characterize those actions and practices derived from our analysis efforts in the context of a comprehensive web strategy. As such, the resulting policies, regardless of their method or use in site optimization all served to foster a more long-term focus relative to our web analytics process. We also demonstrated how our direct actions developed during the analytics process not only impacted short-term performance of the site, but could also be transformed for use in a long-term web strategy through confirmation of success and continued application. Based on this, it appears that the foundation of web or site optimization strategy is complete.

We have a vision defined as the target for our web analytics efforts and through the contribution of each of the various steps, a list of actions and practices that combine to form the direction to be followed.

However, an effective strategy of any kind is one that can be easily communicated to others as a means to unify an entire organization's efforts behind the plan of action that it represents. The action plan or best practices list can both be employed as tools of communication as was alluded to during their introduction. But their value is more evident in their use to confirm action or practice success and foster the evaluation needed to refine them into more stable, long-term policies.

In truth, this process of refinement applied to them in earlier steps mirrors exactly what we are looking to do now. We again need to revisit these various actions, practices and policies from an even broader perspective still and attempt to group them into more general categories and subsequent guidelines. Doing so will organize our "blueprint" into a more cohesive set of objectives with which to target all of our web site operational efforts. We are not suggesting that they be grouped into any of the components of site optimization just described. That information was offered to provide better context around our shift from lists of insights, actions and practices into discussions on web strategy. Instead, we are describing a process that is acting in reverse from where we first started; namely, the identification of objectives and their subdivision into quantifiable, measurable, attainable goals. For this purpose, we have all of the requisite parts and will be "reverse-engineering" them into broader concepts that can be more easily communicated to or enacted by others.

Keep in mind that this act does not render those more detailed actions, practices and policies useless. They will still perform the same roles indicated earlier and remain just as valuable in reference to future reporting periods.

With that said, how do we further refine these lists into a form meant to facilitate better communication? We first look at the vision meant to drive our web strategy. When referenced earlier, we pointed to our web site's original objectives as the suppliers of our own vision or mission. Selling products and increasing revenue translate to being the best or most effective web site relative to these intentions. We next refer back to our lists of actions and best practices and view these as the various tactics employed to achieve our stated mission. What we are looking for now are those strategies that connect the vision to the tactics.

To illustrate, consider again a vision to be the best or most effective e-commerce site. Through the web analytics process, various search engine optimization techniques were employed to improve the site's function and increase sales. Further action was taken through the use of a search engine marketing campaign to increase web site traffic and garner more potential sales. The strategic underpinning of these two tactics relative to achievement of the web site vision can be arrived at as follows.

Both tactics were employed to increase web site sales. One focused on improving the site's structure to better facilitate transactions. The other sought to increase the number of users visiting the site. Why does an improved web site structure increase sales? Because this makes online user transactions easier to perform. How does more visitors equate into more sales? Through the increased sales potential offered by the presence of more users seeking the kind of products the web site offers. The first describes a strategy of providing an environment that makes sales transactions easy. The second describes a strategy to accumulate more of the right type of user audience.

From our tactics derived to achieve our vision, two strategies have emerged to complete their connection. Rather than communicate to others that our strategy is to improve site navigation and run search engine marketing campaigns, we can instead mention that the direction of our web site is driven by a need to ease site usage and target visitors looking for our product offerings. You will note that this process was not unlike the one we conducted to refine our list of best practices. We removed specificity until a more general policy could be attained. We did the same thing in arriving at these strategies except that the removal of any specific aspects was taken one step further.

In essence, we performed a sort of "reverse-engineering" relative to the method used to define our original objectives and goals. Instead of starting with a why, we actually started with the how. How we get more of the right kind of users is performed through SEM campaigns. Why we did this was to get more of the right kind of users to our site.

Perform this step once using one of your existing best practices. If you can come up with a general strategy from it like the example above, see how many other listed practices or policies can be characterized in the same way. You can reference the various components of site optimization to facilitate this effort. Do several pertain to the search engine optimization component? How about user experience? Do these commonalities uncover any shared underpinnings as to why they were implemented? There is no right or wrong answer as to what connects individual tactics, strategies and visions. Any consolidation that can be achieved will contribute to a more cohesive strategy that can be more easily shared and used to unite others.

Again, like so many other aspects of web analytics, this exercise will prove to be subjective depending on the nature of the site, the organization and the original objectives and goals that have dictated all of our efforts to date. Your conclusions as to what strategies drive the tactics discovered through or employed by your own web analytics process will exude a high degree of subjectivity as they are meant to filter communication through your own unique perspective. Regardless, the presentation of the concepts behind this exercise serves as a warm-up for our final discussion on web analytics and the formation of a web strategy. Web analytics, its results, insights and actions and their connection to a wider strategy are part of a continuous cycle that will return us to those first steps intended to form the basis for everything else that we have done throughout each of our various sessions. As we just referenced those original objectives as the visions defining our strategy, we will soon see how the very process they fostered influences them.

Summary Outline

Web Strategy

- A strategy can be defined as a plan of action designed to achieve a specific vision
- The foundation of a web strategy was being formed by defining a vision and further uncovering the actions and policies needed to achieve its maximum result

Insights, Actions and Policies

- Actions intended to influence performance in the short term can actually prove to be best practices demanding implementation over the long term
- We make the leap to web strategy formation using best practices as a building block
- The best practice and action plan lists can now be viewed as a blueprint of a web strategy

Site Optimization

- Site optimization is defined as the effort to maximize performance through optimal site architecture and effective and efficient resource usage
- Site Optimization strategy is interchangeable with web strategy
- Site optimization strategy is made up of several components including:

  Search Engine Optimization

  Search Engine Marketing

  Display Advertising

  Traditional Advertising and Other External Influences

  User Experience

  Resource Allocation

Site Monetization

- Each component shares the same end, maximization or optimization of performance relative to a web site's objectives and goals (its pre-defined vision)

Long-Term Strategy Communication

- An effective strategy of any kind is one that can be easily communicated to others
- It serves as a means to unify an entire organization's efforts behind the plan of action that it represents
- Organize our "blueprint" into a more cohesive set of objectives with which to target all of our web site operational efforts by identifying underlying strategies

Recommended Exercises:

1. Connect objective visions to action and best practice tactics by identifying the underlying strategies that connect them.

2. Combine results to form a web strategy overview.

Chapter 12

Coming Full Circle

Characterizing the web analytics process as a cycle

Coming Full Circle

Throughout many sections of this book, we have demonstrated the idea that each of the different steps we have followed are interconnected and procedures performed further into the process can shed new light on older assertions resulting in adjustments or new areas of focus. In particular, the original objectives and goals documented in step one were referenced in this fashion on more than one occasion.

At the end of the last section, we alluded to web analytics and web strategy as being dynamic and that their execution and formation represented a continuous cycle. Further, we stated that these endeavors would culminate in a return to our very first steps. Next, we will do just that and complete this newly defined cycle connecting our web strategy formation efforts back to our original objectives and goals.

The Complete Web Analytics Process Walkthrough

Let us start by taking a look at the whole process. First, we began by identifying the original reasons why we built the site in the first place. We took these objectives and broke each of them down further in order to determine specific direct actions or indirect engagement activities that could be defined as goals. Their quantifiable, measurable and understandable nature was reviewed to ensure their proper use as an indicator of performance relative to the higher level objectives.

A mapping of the site was recommended to help locate where these goals were actually taking place and to improve understanding of the site's function from a user's perspective. A series of metrics and related data sources were chosen to measure them and were further confirmed as Key Performance Indicators relative to their importance in measuring results and to focus our web analytics efforts.

Next, we organized our data and compared current performance to historical data by means of established baselines and material levels of change. We focused a more intensive analysis on these KPI fluctuations with the intent of discovering cause and effect relationships that could explain their occurrence and lead us to insights improving our understanding and creating an actionable list to influence future results.

From these actionable insights, we began the formation of a wider web strategy by looking deeper into their future implications as a series of best practices, rules, baselines, guides, etc. We characterized a web strategy by looking at site optimization and its components providing a new context with which to view our actionable insights in their various forms. Finally, we sought to group these disparate items into a higher level of principles through shared commonalities in purpose and end results. This exercise was done to better facilitate communication of our newly documented strategy and led us to where we are now.

All of these steps represent the web analytics process as it would be for someone performing it for the first time. Exhibit 3 provides a visual representation of what was just summarized.

Exhibit 3: The Completed Web analytic Process Walkthrough

As you can see, the visual representation of the web analytics process relative to its first walkthrough characterizes it as a cycle. As it nears completion, we are once again brought back to the beginning and our original objectives and goals.

Web Analytics As A Cycle

At the end of the last chapter, we looked at our original objectives as components of our web site's vision and sought to bridge the gap between them and our "tactical" actions and practices by identifying underlying strategies. We used information on the components of site optimization to facilitate this endeavor as we looked to organize all of the various actions and practices into a more communicable form. The intended result would be a streamlined web or site optimization strategy that could be applied to unify organization efforts. To complete this process we compare our new groupings once more to the original objectives that led off this process in the first place. It is expected that you should see numerous correlations but what about those that proved difficult to group. Were there some insights, practices or policies that did not align well with any of the original objectives you initially defined?

What to do if there is no correlation whatsoever? One cannot say if this would ever occur given that they were the original starting point governing all of our efforts to date. However, as a dynamic process, web analytics implies that changes can and will occur. Further, structuring our efforts in terms of a cycle imply that once we come full circle, we will inevitably start over and repeat the process. By returning to those original objectives, we are not just seeking confirmation that our site optimization strategy, in its current form, is correct. Instead, we are actively searching for any need to adjust those original objectives and related goals to better reflect the current state of our dynamic, evolving web operations and analytics process.

Objective and Goal Adjustment

That statement leads us back to the beginning of our cycle and a review of the original goals and objectives. Again, we have already alluded to the idea that they are not necessarily static and could change even before this point of the process is reached. This is particularly the case when first getting started in web analytics as many of you are presumed to be.

Another important distinction to make is the fact that some of the steps described as part of the web analytics process occur at regular, periodic intervals. However, we want to be clear that web strategy formation and original objective review and adjustment are not. We will continue to rely on visual representations as a means of clarification with Exhibit 4. It provides an illustration of the web analytics process within a typical reporting period.

Exhibit 4: The Reporting Period Cycle

It can be noted that several of the steps performed during the initial walkthrough are no longer present. They represented steps needed to get started within web analytics. Revisiting data collection or organization can occur down the road but the expectation is that these and other first time steps will no longer be apart of the regular, periodic process.

To illustrate how these intermittent cycles fit within the larger picture, think of them as wheels turning the hands of a clock. The minute hand completes numerous cycles before one complete twelve hour period is complete. Think of your periodic web analytics efforts as the wheel driving that minute hand. Look at your web strategy formation and adjustment of your original objectives as the full 12 hour cycle. Several of the smaller web analytics cycles are completed before the larger web strategy and objective adjustment does.

This same concept is reflected in the cycle representing conversion of insights into actions that lead to further insights (Recall the visual representation of this cycle provided in chapter 10). These processes are not completed within a single reporting period but span across several as more data is accumulated to allow for a higher degree of insight and understanding. These Action/Insight cycles relate to the reporting period cycle in the same manner described in the clock wheel analogy.

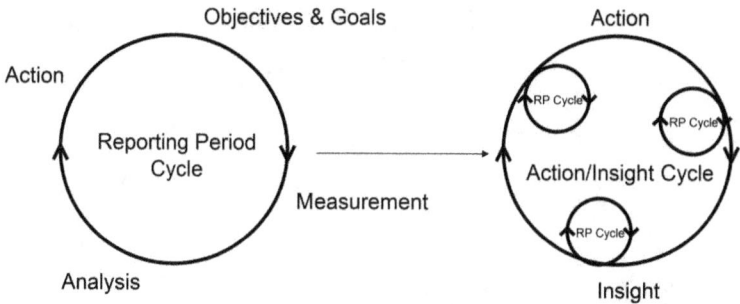

Exhibit 5: The Action/Insight Cycle spanning several reporting periods

This cyclical relationship can be taken another step further by considering the relationship existing between the action/insight cycle and the discovery of new best practices. As successful actions are confirmed, they lead to continued application and eventual discovery and documentation of best practices and policies. This demonstrates yet another clock wheel cycle relationship that is represented below.

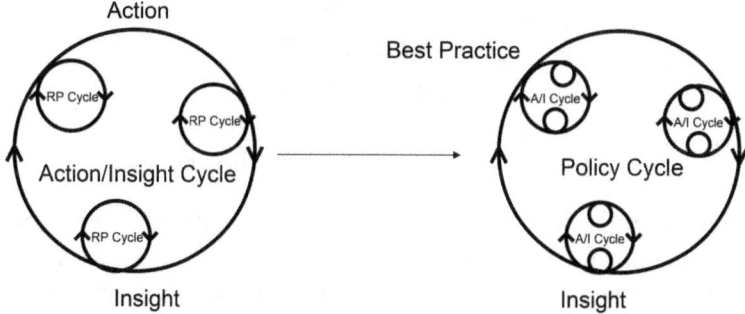

Exhibit 6: Relationship between the Action/Insight Cycle and Best Practice Discovery

The clock wheel analogy has been carried through many of the steps detailed within the web analytics process but has yet to demonstrate how everything fits into the larger picture. Recall the statement from the beginning of this discussion that our return to adjust original objectives and goals do not represent a regular, periodic exercise. Like many of the other cycle relationships just illustrated, the act of objective addition or alteration spans several reporting periods and is itself, characterized using the clock wheel analogy. Each of the other cycles and connections with other, larger spanning cycles all function to complete this final cycle existing between our web strategy formation and the web site objectives.

Objectives & Goals

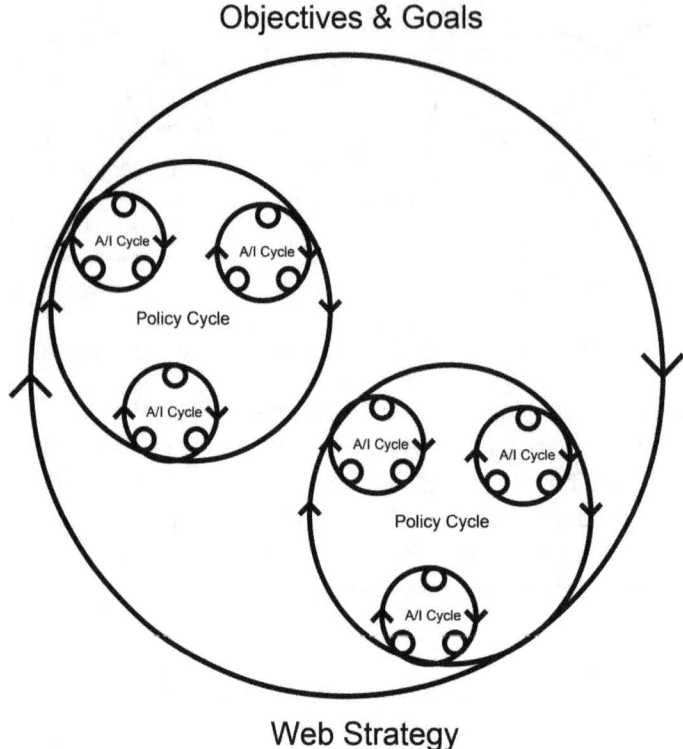

Web Strategy

Exhibit 7: Web strategy leading to objective adjustment

Though not perfect, this clock wheel analogy hopefully reinforces the point that web analytics and all of the related parts we described represent, in their simplest form, a continuous cycle of activity. Like the wheels turning the hands of a clock, each individual cycle is connected to the others, working together until the big hand completes its rotation and the whole process is renewed. Understanding this, you are able to see that all of the steps interconnect in some way, that web analytics and its various components represent a dynamic system and that the web analytics process is never truly complete. Instead, it continues to evolve along with your own understanding and expertise as you work to improve your web site's performance.

Multi-Channel Analytics

Web analytics has now been expressed as an interwoven series of cycles. Each contributes to the movement toward the completion of consecutively higher cycle levels until the starting point is revisited and possibly even changed. Some may argue that this attempt to simplify the array of interrelationships prevalent throughout the web analytics process left out some important aspects. This was necessary in order to avoid being bogged down in too many details as we sought to illustrate the multi-level cycle relationship. However, we can address any concerns through a brief discussion on the concept of multi-channel analytics.

This concept is characterized by its unification of analytics endeavors across a full range of channels into a single, cohesive group. An analytics process like the one presented here can be applied in a separate form to areas that include SEO, SEM and social media in addition to a standard web site. Multi-channel analytics further promotes the idea that digital goals and objectives can be derived from wider organizational marketing efforts to better link online performance to the company as a whole.

Throughout all of our previous discussion, the role of other channels and that of the wider organization were addressed. In some instances, they were tied to our web analytics process in the same manner posited by the concept of multi-channel analytics. There exclusion from any visual representations should not diminish their importance nor invalidate the cycle representation. Given the breadth of our approach, the inclusion of these other channels has likely already occurred. This is especially the case for those readers who brought some experience with them into the process. Those that are new to this will see the relevancy of this concept grow as their own expertise and their online operations evolve.

Regardless, the lesson to be gleaned from the concept of multi-channel analytics is that online performance does not exist in a silo. It can incorporate an array of digital channels and extend beyond to those managed within a wider organization. As the cycle of each channel turns, so does that of your web site and its accompanying strategy. And like the cycle relationship conceptualized earlier, each can be considered an interwoven member of the web analytics process.

Some Final Thoughts

The web analytics process is not unlike the process undertaken to write this book. One starts with the most basic aspects and combines them through a first draft. As each chapter and section is revisited, greater insight is uncovered leading to re-writes, new sections and additional chapters. More information is added that lead to a myriad of changes and additions until the intended scope is achieved. Of course, web analytics has already been described as a continual, ever-evolving process that never really reaches its end. In truth, writing a book attempting to present such a broad and dynamic concept could probably go on in the same fashion. However, some limitations have to be enforced so the reader can move beyond theory and get started on the practice.

We opened this book by citing some common challenges that often preclude someone from getting started with web analytics. It is hoped that at its completion, many if not all have been removed making the idea of jumping into web analytics less daunting. As this was the sole intent of this book, one can reflect on the need to address some very basic steps and ideas. While some more advanced terms and concepts were presented, others were merely referenced or suggested for further study elsewhere. When one considers the vast scope that web analytics can entail, the difficulty in providing detail across every facet becomes apparent. Furthermore, the subjective nature of so many aspects of the web analytics process makes this task even more considerable.

It is with this last thought that we end this book. Applying and learning web analytics techniques represents an evolution unto itself. The deeper one goes, the greater the understanding and the need for further study one encounters. This presentation does not represent a definitive guide to all that may be needed to successfully conduct a web analytics process. However, it does serve as an effective launching point that can and should be supplemented as one's experience and needs evolve.

Summary Outline

Coming Full Circle

- Execution and formation of web analytics and web strategy respectively represents a continuous cycle

- Complete our newly defined cycle connecting our web strategy formation efforts back to our original objectives and goals

The Complete Web Analytics Process Walkthrough

- Each step described throughout this book represents a completed step in the initial web analytics walkthrough

Web Analytics As A Cycle

- Seek to address any actions or practices that could not be tied back to an original objective
- Seeking confirmation of our site optimization strategy and actively searching for any need to adjust those original objectives and related goals
- Common reporting period processes contain fewer steps than those detailed in the initial walk through
- Review and adjustment of objectives spans many reporting periods if it becomes necessary at all
- Many of the other steps within web analytics can be characterized as cycles
- All eventually combine and contribute to this larger, strategy to objective adjustment cycle
- Demonstrates the high degree of interrelationships that exist across the web analytics process

Multi-Channel Analytics

- Address missing or under-represented aspects through a brief discussion on the concept of multi-channel analytics
- The concept is characterized by its unification of analytics endeavors across a full range of channels into a single, cohesive group
- It further promotes the idea that digital goals and objectives can be derived from wider organizational marketing efforts to better link online performance to the company as a whole
- This concept has been addressed, though not specifically throughout our discussion.
- Its relevancy to those that are new to web analytics will emerge as their own process evolves

Some Final Thoughts

- Applying and learning web analytics techniques represents an evolution unto itself
- This presentation serves as an effective launching point that can and should be supplemented as experience and needs evolve

Recommended Exercises:

1. Adjust original objectives to better reflect current state of web site and operational evolution.

Appendix A: Objective and Goal Examples

Objective: Sell products (i.e., mobile phone accessories site)

    Goal: Shopping cart purchases or digital downloads (action)

    Goal: Repeat visitors to site (engagement)

Objective: New client acquisition (i.e., b2b service provider)

    Goal: registration form completions (action)

    Goal: user email submissions (action)

    Goal: phone calls to sales via site specific 800# (action)

Objective: Gather leads/email addresses

    Goal: download of information (action)

    Goal: registration form completions (action)

    Goal: user email submissions (action)

    Goal: phone calls to sales via site specific 800# (action)

Objective: Provide specific/more detailed information to customers - support field sales (i.e., manufacturer's site)

    Goal: download of brochure or product specs (action)

    Goal: user reading (interaction) with specific content (engagement)

Objective: Grow readership (i.e., blog or community site)

    Goal: repeat visitors (engagement)

    Goal: rss feed subscriptions (action)

    Goal: forum comment submissions (action/engagement)

Objective: Drive traffic to another site (i.e., affiliate marketing site)

    Goal: site link clicks (action)

    Goal: new visitors (engagement)

Objective: Site monetization through advertising (i.e., entertainment site)

    Goal: ad clicks (action)

    Goal: time spent on page (engagement)

    Goal: pageviews within specific content page (engagement)

    Goal: garner specific target audience through content (engagement)

Objective: Drive foot traffic to brick and mortar locations (i.e., retail site)

    Goal: Coupon downloads (action)

    Goal: Store Location page views (engagement)

    Goal: Weekly circular views (engagement)

Objective: Distribute content (i.e., news site)

Goal: content interaction, readership (engagement)

Goal: traffic generation from circulated articles (engagement)

Goal: article link clicks (action)

Appendix B: Process Cycle Visuals

The First Web Analytics Walk-through

The Action/Insight Cycle

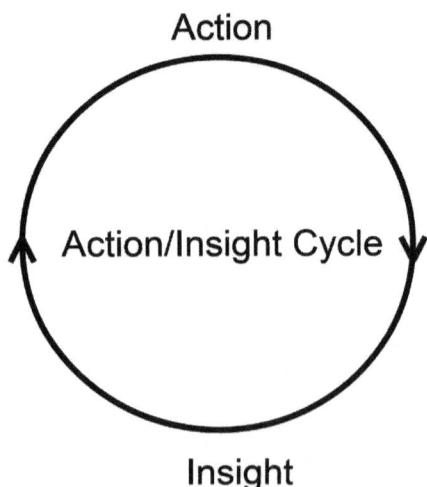

Appendix B: Process Cycle Visuals (continued)

The Regular Reporting Cycle

Relationship Between The Reporting Period and Action/Insight Cycles

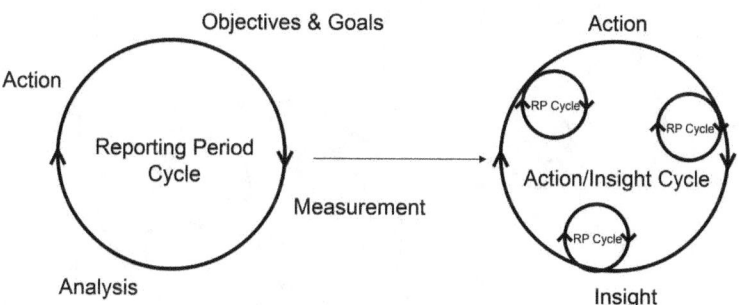

Appendix B: Process Cycle Visuals (continued)

Action/Insight Conversion To Best Practice Policies

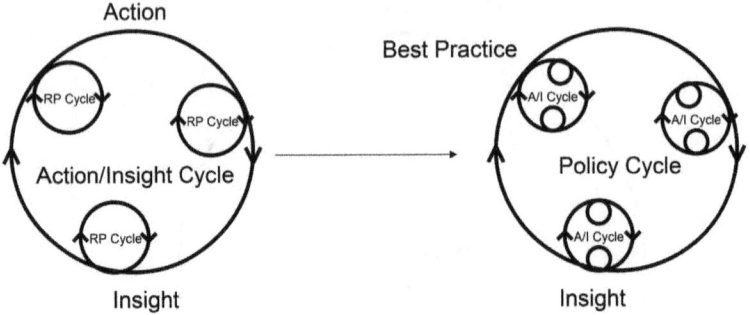

The Web Strategy/Objective Adjustment Cycle

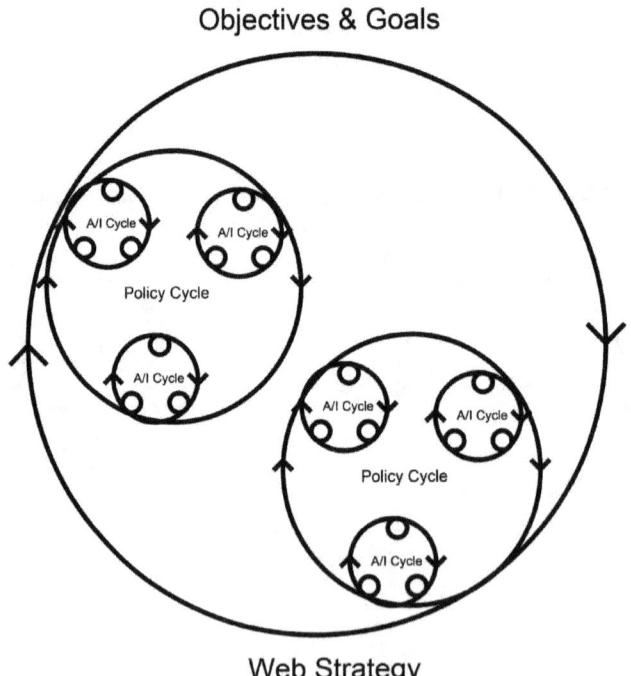

Appendix C: Complete List Of Recommended Exercises

Objective and Goal Definition

1. Document list of defined web site objectives

2. For each objective, define and document related goals pertaining to each

Common Metrics

1. Perform initial assignment of metrics to serve as performance measures of your web site's documented objectives and goals.

Social Media Metrics

1. Review current metric assignments to see if any social media metrics should be added

Data Collection

1. Obtain or create a web site page map

> Include all major site navigation options and sub pages
>
> Connect pages with lines or arrows to demonstrate potential user flow
>
> Include off-site links and note location of ad space

2. Identify sources that will supply results data for all of your web site's objectives, goals and their assigned metrics.

Key Performance Indicators

1. Review existing metric assertions using the more stringent KPI definition and details

2. Design and select new key performance indicators as needed

Organizing Data

1. Organize data into monthly increments

2. Consolidate monthly reports into a centralized worksheet

Measurement

1. Calculate conversion rates.

2. Calculate any needed standard performance baselines for each KPI.

Quantitative Analysis

1. Identify any material levels of change that may be evident within the current reporting period results.

2. Seek to identify cause and effect relationships that explain why those results occurred through analysis of quantitative data.

Qualitative Analysis

1. Continue to perform cause and effect analysis using qualitative data to complete any unresolved investigations.

Taking Action

1. Review all newly discovered cause and effect relationships and convert insights into actionable items. When none can be derived, review your original assertions as some action or best practice should be produced.

2. Document all actions and best practices in a list.

3. Document and review each best practice in order to reflect a more high level policy.

4. Add newly confirmed successful actions to the best practices list in the form of new, high level policies.

Strategy Formation

1. Connect objective visions to action and best practice tactics by identifying the underlying strategies that connect them.

2. Combine results to form a web strategy overview.

Cycle Completion

1. Adjust original objectives to better reflect current state of web site and operational evolution.

ABOUT THE AUTHOR

John Cassidy is a seasoned industry professional with over thirteen years of digital experience in web analytics, marketing strategy, web site management, product development and sales. He has been employed in a variety of online marketing and analytics positions with some of the most well-known web brands in the world including AOL, Mapquest, Netzero, Citysearch.com, Games.com, AIM, Shopping.com and Patch.

John's project, campaign and analytics work has encompassed a full range of organizations from the Fortune 50 to hyperlocal businesses. He has also served as a digital consultant assisting small and medium sized organizations with the development and implementation of their web analytics and other digital marketing processes.

John has a Bachelors degree in accounting from Michigan State University and a MBA in marketing and information systems from Wayne State University. John also has experience as a Certified Public Accountant and is a certified JONAH with expertise in the Theory of Constraints and its various aspects. He draws upon an extensive range of digital marketing and client consultation experience and is an expert in developing and implementing processes that are both efficient and effective. John advocates the belief that anyone can successfully enter the web analytics world given a simple, straightforward place to begin. He also recognizes the importance of solid quantitative and qualitative data analysis in support of key business decisions.

John can be contacted at his web site, http://www.what-is-web-analytics.yolasite.com

www.ingramcontent.com/pod-product-compliance
Lightning Source LLC
Chambersburg PA
CBHW051501170526
45166CB00001B/330